"I want them not to be lonesome tonight."

Be Elvis!

A GUIDE TO IMPERSONATING THE KING

RICK MARINO

WITH ADAM WOOG

SOURCEBOOKS, INC.®
NAPERVILLE, ILLINOIS

Published by Sourcebooks, Inc.
1935 Brookdale Road, Suite 139, Naperville, Illinois 60563.
(630) 961-3900
Fax (630) 961-2168

Be Elvis! A Guide to Impersonating the King is produced by
becker&mayer!, Ltd.
www.beckermayer.com

Design by Two Pollard Design. Art direction by Simon Sung.
Edited by Stephanie Westcott and Sarah McCormic. Production by Marypat Faraone.

Library of Congress Cataloging-in-Publication Data

Marino, Rick.
     Be Elvis! : a guide to impersonating the King / Rick Marino.
          p.   cm.
     Includes discography.
     Includes filmography.
     Includes bibliographical references.
     ISBN 1-57071-556-4 (alk. paper)
     1. Elvis Presley impersonators—Vocational guidance. 2. Elvis Presley
impersonators—Handbooks, manuals, etc. I. Title.
     ML3795.M176 2000
     792.7'028--dc21   00-026582

Printed in China
ISBN 1-57071-556-4

becker & mayer! 10 9 8 7 6 5 4 3 2 1

First Edition

To Trevor
"My Boy! My Boy!"

Table of Contents

Be Elvis!

CHAPTER ONE

Introduction:

Elvis Impersonators

and

How I Became One

You know that old saying about how imitation is the highest form of flattery? Well, it's true when it comes to Elvis Presley, the King of Rock and Roll.

I'm not just talking about somebody standing in front of a bedroom mirror, holding a guitar made from a broom and lip-synching to one of Elvis' albums. And I'm not just talking about musicians who want to capture some of the King's sound for their own.

No, I'm talking about full-blown Elvis impersonators, men (and a few women) who are dedicated to re-creating the King in all his glory. Only a handful make their livings doing tribute-to-the-King shows, but there are thousands—one estimate says 3,000, another 10,000—who are full- or part-time Elvis impersonators.

Now that Elvis is dead, I'm sad to say, these impersonators are as close to the Real Thing as anybody's ever going to see. And with the help of this book…you, too, can be Elvis!

By impersonating Elvis, I help keep the King's passion alive.

Passion On Stage and Off

If I had to describe Elvis' appeal in a single word, I'd say it was *passion*—he had passion about everything he did. No matter what he did in life, on stage or off, he was passionate about it. I believe the world related to this passion—and also to his sincere kindness of heart and genuine concern for others.

Elvis was raised to always have dignity, respect, and compassion, despite his family's terrible poverty. His father, Vernon Presley, gives us an insight into that in this passage from Peter Guralnick's book *Last Train to Memphis*:

"'I told Elvis,' said Vernon, 'that I'd work for him and buy him everything I could afford. If he had problems, he could come to me and I'd try to understand. I also said, 'But, son, if you see anything wrong going on, promise me you'll have no part of it. Just don't let anything happen so that I'd have to talk to you between bars. That's the only thing that would break my heart.'

"'There were times we had nothing to eat but corn bread and water,' recalled Vernon not long before he died,' but we always had compassion for people. Poor we were, I'll never deny that. But trash we weren't….We never had any prejudice. We never put anybody down. Neither did Elvis.'"

Elvis Impersonators Everywhere

The presence of thousands of Elvis impersonators in the world today just emphasizes Elvis' amazing popularity, even decades after his death. It's incredible to realize this, but Elvis is in some ways even more talked about and widely accepted now than when he was alive! His records and movies sell more than ever, his home is the second-most-visited house in the U.S. (after the White House), and it's been said that his face has been reproduced more times than anyone else's.

It doesn't matter who you talk to—movie stars, millionaires, aristocrats, educated people, uneducated people, people who never saw Elvis, foreigners—*everybody* still talks about Elvis. There may not be any other twentieth-century figure who's been photographed more, had more books written about him, or had more things said about him. Elvis has become an international icon. Even before Elvis' death, people were already imitating him, paying tribute to his talents as a performer in shows of their own. Elvis knew about these imitators and liked them; he never had a problem with people impersonating him. (There's even a story, though I don't know how true it is, that Elvis once let an impersonator get onstage with him.)

I think Elvis found it flattering that people thought enough of him to emulate him. He also thought it was amusing and a little embarrassing; he couldn't understand why anybody would want to go around imitating him.

I'll tell you something interesting: his favorite impersonator was Andy Kaufman, the edgy, off-the-wall

Elvis impersonators appeared at both the 1984 Los Angeles Olympics and the 1988 Seoul Olympics.

comedian who often impersonated Elvis on *Saturday Night Live* in the seventies. Elvis *loved* Andy Kaufman! He just flat out thought it was the greatest thing. I've got a tape recording of Elvis publicly acknowledging how cool he thought Andy Kaufman's imitation was.

These impersonators are an important part of the Elvis mystique, keeping his legend alive, and they come in all varieties. There are black Elvises, female Elvises, child Elvises, Hispanic Elvises, Sikh Elvises, Asian Elvises. There are parachuting Elvises and father-and-son Elvises.

Some impersonators have legally changed their names to variations of Elvis', and some have even undergone plastic surgery to resemble him better. You can find these impersonators all over the world: in Las Vegas, Chicago, New York, L.A., and lots of other places—even overseas, in countries like Australia, Japan, Israel, Russia, and England.

I'm one of them. My name's Rick Marino, and I've been performing my "Elvis Extravaganza Show" professionally for over twenty years.

Also, I'm proud to say, I was elected by my peers as the first (and current) president of a worldwide organization dedicated to carrying on Elvis' tradition: the Elvis Presley Impersonators International Association.

Elvis impersonator Robert Washington.

Elvis World

Elvis is everywhere, and everybody knows who he is. Not many people are recognized all around the world by just their first names. Writers Jane and Michael Stern point out this amazing phenomenon in their book celebrating the Elvis legend, *Elvis World*:

"Elvis World is not one place. It is the universe defined by all he stands for: music, of course, and movies, but also the cascade of material things he consumed, the fans he enraptured and stuffed shirts he outraged....

"Gossip mongers relish Elvis. But tabloid slander is not the true road into Elvis World. To get mired in the dirt is to miss the exaltation. Whatever his health problems, they were scrupulously kept private when he was alive. And now that he is dead, they are nothing more than a banal footnote to a career that was extraordinary in every other way.

"There was a time when he was merely the most popular entertainer in history. He is more than that now. He is a symbol of America as recognizable as the flag. Show his picture to a taxi driver in Thailand or a housewife in Tasmania or a ten-year-old child in Bangor, Maine, and they will all recognize him. While working on this book, we never once met anyone who asked, 'Elvis who?' "

Elvis Has Left the Building

Elvis is so beloved that there are persistent rumors that he's still alive. It's as though some people love him so much that they can't believe he was a mere mortal.

Now, I want you to understand something: I firmly believe that *Elvis is dead.* He's sung every song he's ever going to sing, made every move he's ever going to make, done every record and every movie he's ever going to do. *He's not here anymore.* He has left the building for the last time.

That means that you can watch Elvis videos all you want and you can listen to Elvis records forever. But to get anything like the excitement of experiencing a live Elvis show, you'll have to witness an Elvis impersonator.

That's not to compare an Elvis impersonator to Elvis himself, because in my opinion there will never be any greater entertainer. No, an impersonator's show is just a simulation of what it was like...but sometimes it can be a damned good simulation.

Make no mistake about it—we impersonators are not (and never will be) Elvis. We impersonators are not even celebrities. But sometimes we do get close...and that's the fun of it all. Elvis impersonators get the experience and benefits of being a celebrity without the terrible cost of fame—which, as history has so often shown us, can take a tremendous toll.

Elvis' performances thrilled audiences around the world. Now that he's gone, fans can only experience a live Elvis show by watching impersonators.

Here's a strange fact for you: up until just a few years ago, none of your die-hard Elvis fans would have anything to do with Elvis impersonators. The real thing was still too strong a memory, I guess. Once Elvis had been dead for about fifteen years, though, everybody started changing their tune—they started missing him too much, and they realized that the only way to get the live experience of seeing Elvis was through an impersonator.

The Power of Being Elvis

Later in this book, I'll talk more about what it's like to be an Elvis impersonator, and tell some stories about my experiences. For now, I'll just say this:

An incredible thing happens when I go from being Rick to being Elvis. When I'm in costume, everywhere I go, *I am Elvis!* And I can do almost anything I want to do.

In costume, I feel the power Elvis had, the overwhelming effect he possessed over people. I can go into almost any building without question, and people are just awe-struck—I honestly believe I could almost walk right into the White House! It's just unbelievable, and it's even more unbelievable that a person today, so long after Elvis' death, still can dress up like him, walk into a room or a building or a stadium, even the Olympics, and stop everyone in their tracks. Even if it's only for a moment as they say... "Hey, is that *Elvis*?" They know it's not, of course, but still they wish that by some miracle it was.

This power we impersonators have says a lot about Elvis and his continuing fame, popularity, historical value, and mythology. Hey—it's all about Elvis, and like it or not, an Elvis impersonator becomes the vessel that keeps Elvis in the present tense.

The American Dream

In his introduction to *The Elvis Reader*, writer Kevin Quain points out Elvis' unique combination of personas. Elvis represented so many sides of America itself, both what we were and what we are, what we dreamed about and what we really are today:

"He is as much a tribute to the essential optimism of the American Dream as he is an indictment of its falseness and its pitfalls....Few figures in American history have evoked the extreme responses Elvis Presley has, and fewer still have endured after death as a myth, an industry, and a cult figure to the degree Elvis Presley has. Whether Elvis' achievements as an artist or a human being warrant this type of treatment is debatable, but his status as a unique cultural phenomenon is undeniable."

Can't Help Falling in Love with Elvis

People often ask me: "Why? Why do Elvis impersonators exist? And why would anyone want to be an Elvis impersonator?"

One answer to this last question, for sure, is that there's good money to be made. But there's a lot more to it than that. There's the responsibility of keeping Elvis' music legacy alive. There's a spiritual connection

Elvis' hold on our hearts remains strong.

as well—not to mention how much fun it is. I mean to tell you the truth…being Elvis is a blast!

In the end, though, it is really impossible to understand or explain Elvis impersonators. Being Elvis means something different to every one of us, just as Elvis himself meant—and still means—something different to each of his fans.

All I can say is why I started doing it: because I grew up with Elvis and loved him, and I wanted more than anything to maintain his legacy.

I almost can't remember a time before Elvis was there for me—it seems like he's always been part of my life. In fact, I'm told that when I was very young, still in the crib, I actually met Elvis.

When I was a baby, my family lived in Tampa, Florida, next door to some relatives of Colonel Parker's wife. (Colonel Tom Parker was Elvis' manager.) Real early in Elvis' career, when he was just getting started, Colonel Parker brought Elvis to Tampa, and one day they were visiting the Colonel's relatives. These relatives asked my mom if she wanted to come meet Elvis, so she brought me over.

My mom remembers Elvis was sitting there with a couple of his buddies while reporters asked him questions. Elvis would snap his fingers and point, and one of his buddies would answer for him: "Well, Elvis thinks…" My mom thought it was funny that Elvis gave them all equal time. She says Elvis "seemed like a nice young man," but that he talked real mushmouthed, like a real hillbilly—nothing like what he became later.

Apparently he got bored after a while and told his buddies he wanted to go outside and play some football. So they all jumped up, and on the way out I guess I was screaming and crying and pitching a fit. Elvis picked me up and looked at me and said something like, "This kid sure makes a lot of noise!" Then he set me down and went on outside. Not much of an encounter—but they say that if you ever were touched by Elvis, nothing would be the same afterward.

Elvis loved to play football.

The Importance of Being Elvis

People today tend to forget why Elvis should really be famous. In life and in death, he was (and is) famous for being famous. The endless, tacky stories about his fame—his lavish mansion and lifestyle, his epic eating and drug binges, his girls and his parties—often contain some truth, but they've mushroomed over the years to ridiculous extremes.

They also cover up Elvis' very real role in American popular music, and his enduring place as a singer, artist, and entertainer.

Elvis didn't invent rock and roll. He didn't write his own songs (as other classic rockers often did). And you could argue (though I'd disagree!) that he was not rock-and-roll's greatest performer.

Still, he was *the single most important person* in rock music's entire history.

First of all, he popularized rock and roll, making it accessible for the first time to a widespread, mainstream audience. In an era of otherwise bland, safe pop, he was the king rocker—he blew everybody else right out of the water.

He also acted as a bridge between musical styles that had long been strictly segregated along racial lines, mixing black R & B with white country and gospel in a way no one had heard before.

And he was the powerful symbol of the postwar era's rebellious teenage generation. He split America in half: you hated him or you loved him. No matter where you stood, he couldn't be ignored. And he's stayed that way ever since, with no one even coming close. John Lennon once said, "Before Elvis there was nothing," and Bruce Springsteen added, "There have been other contenders, but there is only one King."

Elvis starred in the 1961 film Blue Hawaii.

My next encounter with Elvis—the first time I really became aware of him—happened because of a crush I had on a girl.

This was in 1961 when I was only about eight years old. The daughter of my mother's best friend desperately wanted to see Elvis' movie *Blue Hawaii*. She was thirteen or fourteen and very pretty, and I still remember her name—Donna Brown. I volunteered to accompany her—not for the opportunity to see Elvis, but for the chance to sit next to her in a dark theater for two hours.

Well, we ended up sitting through that film six times! And I was happy to do it. It wasn't just because of the girl—it was because I was in awe of how cool he was. I was fascinated by everything about him—how he looked, how he fought, how he wore his hair, how he sang.

Plus, the enthusiastic reaction of all the people in the theater to everything that Elvis did left a lasting impression on me...especially how the girls just screamed for him. I could see how much he was adored by others. In the third grade, when the teacher asked everybody what they wanted to be when they grew up, all the other kids were saying "policeman," "fireman," or "just like my mom or dad." I said, "I want to be just like Elvis!" I meant that I wanted to be liked and admired by everybody.

Things just went on from there—from my disastrous first performance, through a career as a music producer, promoter, and singer, to my current status as full-time Elvis impersonator.

Getting to this point has been a long, slow, and painstaking process. There were lots of things to learn—and believe me, I'm still learning. Still, my knowledge rests on a foundation of good, solid basics—which is where this book comes in.

I'll be frank with you: I'm not going to tell you everything. I have to keep a *few* secrets to myself! But I am going to share with you plenty of the elements you need to know if you want to "be" Elvis.

So let's get started!

From the very beginning, Elvis' sound and style drove audiences wild.

Elvis had a slight stutter that appeared when he was nervous.

In scenes of *Wild in the Country* and *Kissin' Cousins*, you can hear him stutter slightly.

Be Elvis!

CHAPTER TWO

Hair and Makeup—

Getting the Elvis Look

Elvis had some happening hair his whole life.

For some reason, Elvis apparently didn't like to shower more than he had to. But he always smelled great. This may have had something to do with his favorite cologne, Brut by Fabergé™.

Here's the rundown on some of his other favorite products:

For a dazzling smile: Colgate™ toothpaste

For great hair: Wella Balsam™ shampoo

For silken skin: Neutrogena™ soap

For sweet breath: Scope™ and Listerine™ mouthwash

The first leg on the road to success in being Elvis is to get The Look—and the beginning step in your expedition is to work on your hair and face. Get the hairstyle and the makeup right, and you're on the road to becoming a fine Elvis impersonator.

The Hair: Elvis Started at the Top!

Premier hairstylist Vidal Sassoon was once quoted as saying that Elvis never had a decent haircut in his life. Hogwash! Elvis had some happening hair his whole life.

His early hairstyle—slicked back, with a ducktail and long sideburns—was inspired in part by Tony Curtis and Dean Martin, entertainers he admired as a teenager, and in part by the style favored by truck drivers he saw around Memphis.

He'd started wearing his hair that way back when he was still a junior at Humes High School in Memphis. The look was so important to Elvis that he refused to change it when he turned out for football—and the coach kicked him off the team.

If you're after that early greaser look, you'll need plenty of pomade to get the grease in your hair (Elvis' favored brands were Dixie Peach™ and Lover's Moon™, but you'll have to look for others that suit you).

And remember that Elvis didn't dye his hair really deep black black in the beginning. This may or may not be a surprise, but the King's hair color was not natural. Elvis was born a dirty blond (like the wig he wore in the 1964 film *Kissin' Cousins*).

He began dyeing it black when he first started appearing in the movies. (Even before he started making movies, though, on stages in his early performance days, the pomade he'd used sometimes made his hair look black.) Remember, his early heroes were all movie stars—he even worked at a movie theater as a teenager. More than anything he wanted to be a matinee idol, and all the matinee idols at the time had black hair and blue eyes—like Clark Gable, Rock Hudson, Tony Curtis, and Tyrone Power. He wanted to be a movie star all along, even more than a live performer, and he just got that look locked in his mind. He kept dyeing because it looked so good on film—when he started making movies is when he started dyeing it really deep black. Even in his earliest movies, though, you can see that his hair wasn't jet black—if you look at the movies he made before he went in the Army, there was only a little dye.

When Elvis started seriously dyeing his hair, he became a big fan of L'Oreal Preference™ "Blue Black" dye. That made it the dark black you see in the films. He changed the color of his dye to a more natural-looking soft black for the 1973 *Aloha from Hawaii* concert (which you can see on video), and he continued to use that color till his death. I've heard rumors that a new hair-dye product is coming out with Elvis' name on it, so keep an eye out!

Some say Elvis was inspired to dye his hair black by the deep, deep black hair of Roy Orbison, a singer Elvis greatly admired.

Finding a Good Hairstylist

As far as I know, Elvis only had two people do his hair throughout most of his career: his good buddy Charlie Hodge (who was also his band director) and, later, Larry Geller (who was a big influence on Elvis' interest in spiritual matters). Let this be a lesson: once you find stylists you like, stay with them, if at all possible. I've only had seven different stylists cut my hair over the last twenty-eight years, and their shears have been so central to my look that I can still remember each and every one by name.

It's very important to find a hairstylist who has been cutting hair for twenty years or so, because the cut you need isn't like the cuts that stylists do today. For instance, there's Elvis' seventies style haircut. It's very hard to duplicate that, and you really have to have some knowledge and experience. You see, back in the seventies they used to cut front to back; nowadays they cut back to front, and it creates a different effect. If you're striving to achieve the look of Elvis during his younger days, the advice is still the same: find somebody who knows how to cut hair in the way you want.

Most stylists will be excited at the opportunity to really go retro; after all, this isn't a cut they get to do every day. To guide their shears, it's always a good idea to bring in plenty of photos of Elvis as examples. No matter how talented the stylist, photos to use as guides will come in handy.

Once the stylist shapes your hair and you're satisfied with it, almost any stylist can do the upkeep, so long as they follow the lines of your existing cut. Be firm about this. My current stylist still doesn't get my hair quite right from time to time, but she does understand that I'm very particular about my do. You should be, too, and the reason is as obvious as the hair on your head: to be taken seriously as an Elvis impersonator, you have to be definite about The Look.

I suggest that you only get a cut every three to four months, with only a slight trim—very slight!—if necessary in between. Hair is so important to your overall look that you may want to plan a haircut a month or so before a big show.

Dye—for Both Your Head and Body

Unless you're lucky enough to have naturally black hair, you're going to want to dye it when you start on your Elvis look. Hair on the head can be dyed two different ways: temporarily or permanently. Personally, I suggest temporary; it looks more natural, is a lot easier on hair (mostly because it doesn't have ammonia), and rinses out gradually, making it a lot less noticeable as it grows out—so there are no roots!

There are two kinds of temporary dye I prefer: those that last six to twelve shampoos, and those that last through twenty-four shampoos and are almost like a permanent dye. The twenty-four-shampoo dye is easier to apply; however, I recommend using the more forgiving six-to-twelve type. I personally use the longer-lasting product only for convenience, when I know I'll be gone from home longer than ten days doing shows.

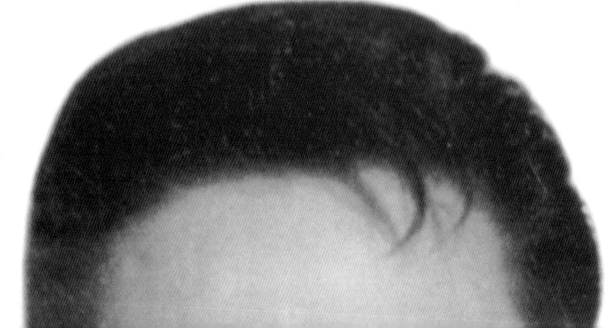

Dyeing to be the King

Have all your stuff ready before you start dyeing, so you don't get caught unprepared. If possible, have someone help you. (My sister-in-law usually helps me. I go over to her place, and it takes about an hour.) You'll need a latex glove, a small brush like a mustache brush, tissues, and a small mixing cup (plastic or porcelain).

When dyeing, run water in the sink and stand in front of the bathroom mirror. Always dye shirtless and *before* showering, not after. It's better for your hair, the chemicals don't saturate the hair too much, and it comes off your skin easier. Also, taking a shower afterwards gives your hair a more natural look. Enough of the dye hangs on your hair to darken it, but some will wash off. Truthfully, that's a big secret—people think that the more pure and darker black their hair is, the better Elvis they'll be; but it just looks more unrealistic.

The Army uniform of Private Elvis Presley.

The Most Photographed Haircut in History

In 1957, the U.S. Army gained one of its most famous soldiers: Private Elvis Presley.

Elvis refused to let his manager pull strings to get him special treatment. Despite his wish to be treated like any other soldier, though, Elvis' first days of Army life at Fort Chaffee, Arkansas, were a circus, with his slightest move recorded by dozens of photographers and reporters. One photographer even tried to hide in the barracks to get a snapshot of the King in bed!

One ritual that any new soldier undergoes was especially significant for Elvis: the buzz cut.

Elvis' Army cut was surely the most photographed, most written-about haircut in history...and probably the most talked-about since Samson's! While the military barber was trimming away, Elvis smiled for the fifty-five newsmen surrounding him and, as his locks fell to the floor, smiled at the reporters and murmured, "Hair today, gone tomorrow." Then a special detail of soldiers swept up Elvis' hair and destroyed it so rabid fans couldn't get at it.

Keep a little Vaseline™ handy for skin preparation—it helps prevent staining, by protecting areas you don't want stained. You know how, when you're painting something, you use masking tape to protect areas you don't want painted? Same idea. (Note: Don't wait to wipe off your skin if dye drips—take care of it right away.)

Even though the directions say to leave it on for five minutes, I've found thirty minutes to be more effective. When the process is complete, step into the shower, rinse off, and hope it's right! The color should last two to three weeks, depending on your individual rate of hair growth. Between dyes, mascara can be used for touch-ups; mostly you'll need these on the temples and sideburns. (Make sure you always use water-based makeup, for easy cleanup and preservation of your costumes.)

I always use a natural black color. The brand my stylist recommends is Clairol's Loving Care™—he says there are absolutely no chemicals in it that will hurt your hair. Now they've got a new version of Loving Care that lasts as long as a couple of months instead of a couple of weeks. I'd recommend you go that route if you need your hair colored for an extended period of time because of a busy schedule or travel.

Between dyes, use mascara for touch-ups.

Touch-ups are most important on the temples and sideburns.

Your Elvis do is complete!

"His Hair Is His Crowning Glory"

In their book *Elvis World*, Jane and Michael Stern poetically describe Elvis' appearance in a typical early performance. Their description gives a good idea of the importance of having good makeup and hair.

"His face is as startling as his body. In repose, the profile is Michelangelo's David: classical Grecian nose flattened and straight as a rule, venting hot breath above pouty lips. But it is seldom in repose. The mouth twitches and grimaces, flickering from a sneer to a boyish smile. The eyelids, low and lush, tinted by nature a pale iridescent brown, and by mascara a sooty black, hang heavy over pale blue eyes that shimmy in and out of focus.

"Like buttercream frosting on a cake, his hair is his crowning glory. Depending on the month and the performance, it ranges from light brown to black. What is constant is the great gob of pomade, a glistening brilliantine of good-ol'-boy viscosity like Dixie Peach or Lover's Moon, raked into the locks so thick that you can count the furrows dug by the tines of the comb.

"The tonsorial pyrotechnics are not just a hairdo, no mere wad of mane to keep the head warm and the hat cushioned. Hair is his trademark and his strength. It has a life of its own, more than the sum of the parts that critics inventory and fans dote over—the sideburns, the wave, the fenders, the duck's ass.

"Like the man to whose scalp it is attached, the hair breaks loose onstage. Appearing first as a unitary loaf of high-rise melted vinyl etched with grooves along the side, it detonates at the strike of the first chord. It hangs low and dirty, it whips to the beat, it clings like a greedy lover to the sweaty skin on Elvis' neck."

My Disaster with Permanent Dye

Here's a story to make you think twice before using permanent dye. Before I left for Korea to perform for three months, I decided to try a permanent dye so I wouldn't have to worry about my hair on the road. I knew I'd be doing shows every single night, and I didn't know what kind of supplies or water or anything would be available. So I went to a stylist for a permanent dye, a really black tint like Elvis had in his middle years, because that's what I was going to be doing. I don't know why, but the stylist had to dye my hair three times before the dye took—my hair kept rejecting the product!

A couple of months later, I started losing my hair in clumps, probably due to all the ammonia and other harsh chemicals in the dye. I've got thick, thick hair—I'm Italian, there's not a bald person in my family—and when it started coming out, I was, as you can imagine, pretty upset. The worst was when I went to the beach—the top of my head was sunburned! That freaked me out. You can bet I wasn't wild about the prospect of being a bald Elvis. Fortunately, when I cut it short, it grew back normally.

My hair is thinning a bit now, but that's because I'm five years away from fifty and it's normal. I was lucky, though, that the damage wasn't permanent.

Sideburns

Real ones are the only way to go here. I'll tell you why: I tried stick-on sideburns once, and during a performance, one of them got pulled loose and was hanging and flopping around without me realizing it! I tell you, I was so embarrassed when I realized it after the show.

Nonetheless, you may want to try stick-ons. I understand the varieties available today are much better. I do know some guys who have fake ones. So long as you don't mind spending a little money on high-quality sideburns, they don't have to look bad.

Fitting yourself with artificial sideburns will require going to a professional theatrical shop and having some custom-made, then using a little spirit gum (a solution commonly used by actors to affix fake hair, which should be available in the same shop) to hold them in place. Still, in my opinion, real sideburns give you an authentic look that just can't be beat.

Speaking of illusions—if your hair is naturally thin, you might try a spray designed to give the illusion of thickening it. A lot of stars use a spray around the hairline to give their hair a thicker appearance—Wayne Newton used a spray for years before he finally gave in and went to a toupee. With a lot of stars, on stage it'll look like they've got a full head of hair, but when they go backstage and the light from behind hits them, you can see right through their hair. That's the effect of a spray.

Elvis' Makeup

Everyone is familiar with the image of Elvis' face: his pouty lips, smooth face, smudged-looking sleepy eyes, and long lashes. What may not be as widely known is that the King had a heavy hand when it came to makeup, particularly eyeliner and mascara. He knew, as every Elvis impersonator should know, that makeup is very important.

Elvis wore makeup even back in the fifties. He was a big movie buff all his life, and as a teenager he admired many entertainers—as I've said, he was especially a fan of Dean Martin and Tony Curtis. He liked the way they looked on screen, and Dino's laid-back cool was a major influence. Elvis studied the way Dean and Tony wore their hair, and how Tony wore makeup, with his eyelashes done up with mascara. Elvis used other kinds of makeup, too—eye shadow, for instance, to give him a brooding look.

He also used makeup to smooth out his complexion. He'd had a lot of problems with acne when he was a teenager, and his face was rather pitted. Later in life, after he started making movies, he had several peels and things of that nature.

Elvis also had large pores on his skin, and as he got older he used makeup to smooth those out. He did other things too—sometime in late '74 or early '75 he had a little plastic surgery on his eyes and lids. When they do that they cut in your eyebrow, and so his eyebrows were real thin at the end of his career. He'd dyed them for years, but in the videos made toward the end of his life, especially the last one, *Elvis in Concert*, you can see that he's drawn his eyebrows on. He used a heavy brow pencil to make his thinner eyebrows look fuller.

As he got older, Elvis used mascara on his sideburns, too. His sideburns started going white after he turned about forty, and he used mascara along the edge of the sideburns to cover the white. I have to do this myself. I'd have to dye my sideburns every single day to hide the gray! Instead, when I'm doing a show I use a little mascara with my personal favorite, Maybelline™ Velvet Black.

Elvis used makeup as far back as the fifties, imitating movie stars like Dean Martin and Tony Curtis.

After you've worked on getting your hair and face right to your satisfaction, the next step is to work on your clothes. In my opinion, the proper threads are just as important to your success as hair and makeup; it's hard work to get it right, and it'll cost you a few dollars, but the result is well worth it.

Don't Cheap Out

Whenever I talk to new impersonators and they ask what my secret is, I tell them the only difference between them and me is the costume. An Elvis show is basically worth what the costume costs.

You can go with a cheap, home-made costume if you really want. But if you really want to do Elvis right, get a job—wash dishes at night if you have to—and invest the extra money in a good costume. That's what I did—I never washed dishes, but I did invest all the spare money I could scrape together in my career.

Many wanna-be Elvis impersonators have misconceptions about what it takes to get started, so let me just lay it down for you nice and clear. I can't emphasize this enough: There is *absolutely no way* to do even the simplest Elvis impersonation for less than a hundred dollars. You can't even *rent* a good Elvis costume for less than a hundred bucks! So a big chunk of your total budget had better go toward getting the costume down. Don't cheap

out when it comes to good clothes. Elvis sure didn't!

On the other hand, there's no need to go overboard here, especially if you're on a tight budget. Obviously, reproducing some of Elvis' outfits is going to require lots of effort and outlay. Others can be reproduced relatively easily and cheaply—and significant savings can be had if you're willing and able to do much of the work yourself. So economize when it seems right.

I never cheap out when it comes to my costumes.

Outfits Through the Years

Later in this chapter, we'll get into details of reproducing a typical costume from Elvis' jumpsuit era, as an example of how to copy specific outfits. First, though, here's a rough breakdown of his different styles through the years, with brief notes.

1950s—The Cat Clothes Era

This is the period when the King was young and wild and wore those great, flashy rockabilly-style threads.

Elvis was a snappy dresser even in high school, before he ever appeared on a stage. He favored flamboyant shirts, pleated trousers, wild sports coats, and bold color combinations, like his favorite: pink and black. He also liked an odd mix of styles, such as a striped sports jacket with a velvet collar that he matched with a pearl-button Western shirt.

Then, of course, there's the famous gold lamé suit seen on the cover of *50,000,000 Elvis Fans Can't Be Wrong*. (This suit was designed in '57 by Nudie's of Hollywood, a costumer to the stars famous for outlandish stylings, and it's now on display at Graceland.) The gold suit and the "Jailhouse Rock" look can both be re-created very cost effectively and relatively easily.

It's doubtful whether Elvis' outfits from this era could be re-created exactly, unless a tailor custom-copied one. But a fine costume in the spirit of this period can be assembled by scrounging in secondhand stores such as the Salvation Army.

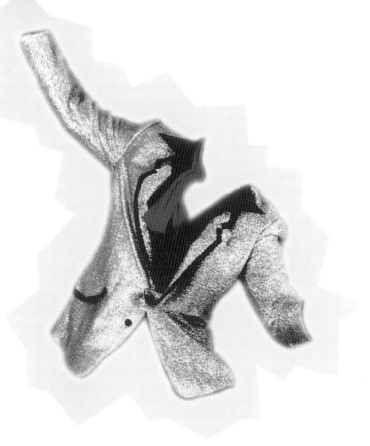

I'd advise an Elvis-impersonator hopeful to get as many picture books of Elvis as possible. Scour and study these books and magazines to find front, back, and side views. Then start hunting. The main ingredient needed here is patience. It's easy to find some good-looking old clothes— an old waiter's jacket, say, or vintage pleated pants—and some of this stuff can also be bought new off the rack, because the style has come back. But I'd still recommend hitting a thrift store, because a lot of money can be saved there. Of course, as success starts to come, so can the tailors and the custom-made clothes.

1967–70—The Black Leather and White Suit Era

Outfits from this era are also relatively easy to reproduce. For instance, the leather "'68 Comeback Special" outfit can be replicated with a minimum of effort and expense using a pair of leather pants and a Levis™ jean jacket that you get reproduced in leather or a synthetic like ultraleather or ultrasuede, with the special addition of a jumpsuit-style collar. (The man who designed this leather suit, Bill Belew, has remarked that the collar was based on those Napoleon wore.)

Other costumes from this era are among the least expensive to reproduce. Many, for instance, were essentially plain white suits with fringe, chains, and a few accessories. They had no kick pleats. The belts fro this period were usually made of macramé cord and are also easy to re-create.

One of the very few Elvis products that did not sell especially well: glue-on sideburns.

Elvis wore:

- His shirt collar up because he was self conscious of his long neck.
- Size 11D or 12D shoes.
- Silk pajamas with E.P. embroidered on them. (Elvis had his initials or those of his motto, Takin' Care of Business, on almost everything he owned.) Elvis owned twenty pairs of pajamas toward the end of his life. When he died, he was wearing pajamas with a blue top and yellow bottoms.
- Elvis never wore jeans, and rarely wore sneakers, because they reminded him of being poor. The only time he wore sneakers was when he played football.

1971–73—The Color Era

This era introduced the first of Elvis' increasingly elaborate color costumes. They came in black, red, royal and powder blue, and even purple! This was also the era of the first studded jumpsuits. Among the designs that the studs made were the pinwheel, owl, star, and starburst.

To match the decoration of the suits, Elvis introduced heavy leather belts with chains, and he also began wearing capes. Looking carefully at these costumes will reveal patterns that produce a specific theme. The patterns are made of basic geometric themes that become filled out with the complexity of the design.

To design your own custom pattern, keep in mind a theme, like Elvis did. I have seen too many suits that came from the "shotgun" school of design—a hodge-podge of nail heads and stones that produce a suit with no theme and no pizzazz.

The nail heads used on the stud designs of these suits were not very heavy, and the shapes used are relatively easy to find. Look for these in costume shops, bead stores, or craft stores. It is cheaper and sometimes necessary to buy nail heads by the "mil"—quantities of 1,000 and multiples thereof.

My First Outfit: Cheap but Effective—at Least for a Nineteen-Year-Old

The better your costume is, the more successful you'll be. Extra effort does get noticed.

I've come a long ways since I made my first costume, which wasn't much more than a denim jacket with an iron-on picture of Elvis on the back. I didn't wear a shirt, left the jacket unbuttoned, and topped it off with skin-tight jeans and, of course, white boots. I was cool—at least I thought I was. Hey, I was only nineteen!

At the time I started, all anybody who wanted to imitate Elvis had to go on were photos, an occasional movie on Sunday afternoon, a few documentaries, or *The Late Late Show*. In those days, long long ago, there were no VCRs, no video, no cable TV, no documentation of any kind. You had to use your imagination, be creative, listen to the music and put pictures in your head to get The Look.

The Late Late Show is where I got the idea for the denim jacket and jean outfit—I had just seen *Loving You*, and if you remember the "Got a Lot of Livin' to Do" scene at the end of the movie, you will see the connection.

To be honest, I never performed much in this outfit—but it was great for a starter costume. The point is that I took the time and put some thought into my presentation, and it made a difference.

Later, when I had the money, I spent several hundred dollars on my black leathers (which I still wear today), modeled after one of Elvis' "'68 Special" costumes. They became my first professional Elvis costume, and they made all the difference in how people regarded me professionally.

1973–75—The Stud and Stone Era

These suits added more splashes of color and glitz to Elvis' show. Themes were elaborated as with earlier styles, created on each suit with a combination of nail heads and cabochons—shiny gem studs. Rim settings were used to further enhance the beauty of the outfit (and their weight—these suckers are heavy).

Cabochons are available in round and oval glass or acrylic, and they come in many different sizes and colors. Many of Elvis' costumes included expensive cabochons called "Aurora Borealis" or "AB" stones. These stones have a rainbow iridescence that makes them flash different colors under stage lighting. Reproducing these costumes is expensive and time-consuming, but still a doable project. These were the last outfits Elvis used with capes.

The Aztec Sundial

While Elvis had a lot of great outfits, one of the best was 1977's "Aztec Sundial" suit. This was the last suit Elvis was seen in, worn during his last performance and in the CBS television special that was shown after he died. Elvis actually wore it more than any other suit he ever owned, although at the time it was not a fan favorite. (He had two of these suits, because of his fluctuating weight condition.) Due to the prohibitive price of making this suit ($5,200, which went a lot farther in the 1970s—that embroidery was expensive!), I only know of three impersonators with this one.

Elvis always dressed with style.

1974–77—The Embroidered Era

These suits are frankly beyond the scope of the average do-it-yourselfer. They represent the pinnacle of the elaborateness of Elvis' costumes, combining the use of nail heads, cabochons, and rhinestones with colorful, intricate embroidery. The embroidery has to be done by a skilled worker using specialized equipment. This is one reason why I say these outfits are beyond the scope of the average do-it-yourselfer. However, I have seen the embroidery effectively reproduced using fabric paint applied with an airbrush.

A 1994 auction of Elvis belongings fetched some handsome sums:

A jumpsuit studded with faux turquoise went for $101,500.

Creating an Elvis-style Jumpsuit

Here's how one of Elvis' costumes—a "late Elvis" look in a jumpsuit—can be reproduced.

First, buy a pattern. Believe it or not, there are a couple of pretty good patterns—Simplicity™ Costumes #8646 "Elvis Elvis Elvis" is the one for children, and there is also one for adults, which you can find in the costume section of the pattern book. These patterns sell for around $10 at fabric shops; sometimes discount stores will also carry fabric and other sewing-related items.

Specific Materials—What to Use

Here's more on the basic materials list for a jumpsuit-style costume. You'll need:

Thread

Studs, beads, and other accoutrements

Depending on how creative you want to be, dressing up your costume with studs and beads could cost $20 and up.

Polyester gabardine

Many of Elvis' original costumes were made of Italian gabardine, but this is hard to find, expensive, and extremely hot to wear. Polyester gabardine works fine: it wears better, is moth-proof, and won't mold when put away damp from sweat. (Always take the time post-performance to hang up damp costumes to dry so that they don't mildew.) Plus, it's much less expensive: polyester gabardine can be found at around $5 a yard,

while Italian gabardine is $60 a yard and up. You'll need about 4 yards for a jumpsuit and another 2 yards for the cape.

When choosing a gabardine, look for material with a good weight and some stretch. Polyester gabardine is normally available in assorted colors, including white, off-white, red, black, royal blue, black, and hard-to-find powder blue. So you're bound to find something that looks good.

Note: Be selective—and creative—when choosing a color. The lady who makes my scarves gave me an important tip here: everyone has a hue that matches his or her particular complexion, so certain scarves and collars will look good on that person, but others won't. For instance, I look good in purple but terrible in brown. Experiment and learn what your colors are, based on your complexion.

Shop around at your local fabric store, and if you can't find what you need, see if the shop can order it for you. If that doesn't work, check the Yellow Pages in the nearest large city. Call around and ask for samples and see if they will send it to you.

Tricot or Antron nylon underknit

This fabric is excellent for lining the inside of costumes, if you decide to do that. (You don't really have to, but it'll give you a better-quality result.) The nylon is light, stretchy, and breathes well. It's generally available in white, off-white, black, and shades of red and blue. You'll need about 4 yards.

Polyester satin

Elvis' costumes always had matching inserts in the collar, lapel, and kick pleat. (The kick pleat is the colorful slash on the lower outside pant leg. This varies in length from 12 to 17 inches and around 4 inches wide at the bottom.) Pick a good weight with a nice sheen. Besides polyester satin, Elvis also used gold, silver, and peacock blue lamé. You'll need about 2 yards.

Zipper

No mystery here. Just make sure it works. Heavy-duty plastic zippers—molded in colors to match the fabric colors—look nice.

Elvis' favorite vacation spot: Hawaii

Put on Your Cat Clothes, Daddy

When Elvis was a teen, he bought his clothes from a Memphis menswear shop called Lansky Brothers. This store was just off Beale Street, the legendary home of the blues and a focal point of Memphis' black community. The patrons at Lansky Brothers were mostly black; the fact that Elvis shopped there, considering the racial segregation common in the South at the time, was radical and daring.

I had the pleasure of meeting Guy Lansky, the man who sold Elvis his suits. I went into a shop in the Peabody Hotel in Memphis, and started talking with a fellow who worked there. We probably talked for a good twenty minutes, and as I was leaving, he gave me his card. I saw that he was Guy Lansky! I said, "I had no idea! What an honor!" It was one of the highlights of my life.

Grommets

You'll need these flat metal "doughnuts" for reproducing costumes that employ ten to fifteen of them on the lapel and collar.

(You'll probably want a tailor to install these. A special setting tool is required, but it's expensive and hard to find. To get around this, use a Dremel tool and a cutting wheel, and serrate the flange at the back of the grommet. Cut seven or eight equally squared slots; this will allow you to bend the resulting tabs over the backing ring easily.)

Check your local costume and fabric stores to find grommets. Another possible source is a tent-and-awning shop, though what you'll find there is made of heavier brass. A tent shop will be able to install the grommets for you as well.

Most grommets are sized $1^1/_2$ diameter with a $^3/_6$-inch hole. These are also available in a square shape. If you can't find silver grommets, you can get brass, nickel-plated ones.

Interfacing

You'll need an assortment of interfacing, preferably nonwoven and medium weight, for collar and lapel stiffness.

Get Measured Right for a Good Fit

If you decide to have your costume custom made, you'll need to find yourself a good seamstress or tailor. (Unless, of course, you're lucky enough to have the skills to do it yourself.)

If you don't have somebody in mind already, look for someone who is well experienced in custom projects and also has good references. Ask to see samples of his or her work and make sure the right equipment is available—principally, a good-quality sewing machine and serger. (The serger is a machine that's handy to keep the costume from fraying on the inside. It's also good for edging scarves.) Your seamstress/tailor should also have experience in drafting a pattern from scratch.

Drafting a pattern won't be cheap! Expect to pay upwards of $150 just to have a pattern drafted for you. (Expect to pay a similar amount for actually making the suit.) Ask if you can buy the pattern, though some may not sell it to you. Patterns are like photographers' negatives—often the tailor or seamstress will make you as many copies as you want, but won't part with the pattern.

The time involved in producing a jumpsuit will depend, of course, on the intricacy of the pattern. A pinwheel design has approximately 1,800 nail heads and will take around twenty hours. Reproducing a more elaborate costume, such as the "Aloha" suit (the one Elvis wore during his worldwide broadcast from Hawaii) with its estimated 5,000 nail heads, can take sixty to seventy hours of work.

Here are some things to look for when drafting a pattern. Getting these details right is important for creating a good-looking, well-cut suit, and can make or break the final result.

Collar

Often collars are too tall, Dracula-style, and too floppy. The satin inserts are installed on the inside of the collar to show through when the grommets are installed.

Here's a tip on collars: You can easily make a cape attachment on the back of the collar with Velcro™. Just place a 5 by 1½-inch strip of Velcro on the back of the collar. Put the matching Velcro strip of the same size onto the top of the cape. Flip up the collar, match up the Velcro strips, and you're in business.

Bell-Bottoms and kickpleats

Elvis' first jumpsuits had a short, narrow 12-inch kick pleat. These evolved over time to become wide bells and knee-high kick pleats. The "Aloha" suit is a fine example.

Again, take the time to get it right so you don't look like a cheap phony. The outside leg seams should have extension flaps on the front and back panel. The kick pleat section is approximately 2 inches at the top and 4 inches at the bottom, regardless of length. When the kick pleat slack is pressed out, leave a half-inch gap at the hemline. This will provide you with an accurate-looking kick pleat.

An Elvis Cologne was marketed in '91 with the tag "For All The King's Men."

Sleeves and cuffs

This is another area where I see many badly cut suits. The seams on the sleeves should be located on the front and back of the sleeve, not on the inside and outside. Seams located on the inside and outside will make the points of the cuff aim inward or outward and look silly. Watch that you don't make the cuff point too pronounced. The length of the sleeve should come down to the first knuckle above the thumbnail.

Front and fly

The "V" of the front neckline should start at the base of the sternum and only go wide to just on either side of the start of the collarbones. The fly should have a pant-style flap to cover on the left side.

Belts

Elvis' belts were 4 inches wide, the buckles 5 to 6 inches high by 7 $\frac{3}{6}$ inches wide, and cut like a gunfighter's belt, so they hung on his hips without slipping but still rode low in front. You should find or make one that will do the same.

Once you've got the jumpsuit in order, it's time to look at your feet....

Generous Elvis

Though Elvis had only a few TCB pins made for special friends and associates, he had many other pieces of expensive jewelry made so he could give them away. In fact, he loved giving away lots of stuff. A good measure of the man is that though Elvis had tons of personal jewelry, he rarely got a chance to wear it because he would give pieces away to the "Memphis Mafia"—his inner circle of friends—or anybody who meant something special to him. When he died, it's said, a TCB necklace he'd given his Aunt Delta had to be "borrowed" back so it could be put on him while his body was on view in his coffin. (I understand it was taken off before he was buried, and returned to her. She has recently passed away, and I don't know who has it—but think how special that necklace is now.)

Put on Your Blue Suede Shoes...

Well, actually, Elvis usually wore white boots, and for the Elvis impersonator, finding the right footwear can present serious problems. Shoes are the number one, most talked-about roadblock and nightmare for all Elvis impersonators. White boots are just not in style, and haven't been for years—so finding a pair can be the most difficult task for Elvises at any level.

Assuming you want to buy a pair, my main piece of advice is to look around. If you are feeling extremely lucky, you can check consignment shops or secondhand stores, but that's a long shot. In the meantime, we're economizing here, so let's go to a tuxedo rental shop and rent some white shoes for approximately $6.

OK! So far your investment amounts to renting or buying shoes; material for the jumpsuit; and maybe about forty hours of your time. But you're far from being done. There are lots of accessories you still need....

The Story Behind "Blue Suede Shoes"

"Blue Suede Shoes" was and still is a Carl Perkins song! Elvis only shared it with the songwriter, and although the press gave Elvis credit for it, he would not have recorded it at all except for the fact that Carl was in a bad auto wreck that seriously injured his two brothers and almost took his life.

While laid up, Carl encouraged his friend Elvis to record the tune...and the rest is history. Despite Elvis' monster success with the song, Carl never complained that Elvis' version outsold his own. In fact, he had reason to thank Elvis, since Perkins received royalties from the song at a time that he really needed them. One interesting thing to note: despite the fact that Elvis' version sold far more copies over time, Perkins' version went to number one, while the King's did not.

Scarves

Scarves were an essential element in the full experience of an Elvis show. His were pure luxury: one full square yard of silk, signed, folded corner to corner, and wrapped around his neck. He'd fling them out into the crowd during certain numbers and the effect of the weight of the scarf floating down was spectacular! But unless an Elvis impersonator has found a cash cow to milk, buying yards of silk to throw away at shows just isn't economical.

Show scarves can usually only be purchased at certain times of year, since scarves are a seasonal item. I suggest looking in discount stores for the best deals. Each "silk" scarf (actually crepe de chine or a similar material) will run about $10.

Or you can make your own. For that, it's back to the discount or fabric store (places any Elvis impersonator gets to know well), where you need to buy some crepe de chine or polyester material with a flat, not shiny, sheen. The material will cost approximately $4 for each. Don't forget while you're there to pick up matching thread.

Pick out a color and have the sales associate cut the material (45 inches wide, 54 inches long). While you're at it, ask them to fudge an inch or two—they will usually cut it 56 inches long. The reason for this is simple: you don't want a short scarf—it's just plain tacky! Some impersonators try to cut cost corners by scrimping, but I tell you, nothing looks more ridiculous than an Elvis impersonator wearing a short scarf with unmatching thread.

When sewn, your scarf should be approximately 8½ inches wide by 54 inches long. Here's a tip: don't try to cut the material into 8½-inch strips. It's more effective to

All good impersonators should incorporate scarves into their shows.

snip the edges ½ or 1 inch along the short edge and then rip it very fast the long way into five equal strips before hemming.

Next, find someone who can sew a hem. My own personal scarfmaker is Mrs. Wonda Vige, who has been making my scarves for me for ten years, and I appreciate it more than I can say—they are such an important part of the show! Making a scarf is very tedious, which is why it's so hard to keep a person making them for you for any length of time.

If you do use scarves in your show, as all good impersonators should, you should take the time to sign them, preferably with a quick-drying silver or gold metallic outlining marker. This creates a glamorous effect and a great souvenir for the lucky fans who get them. If you want to presign them before a show, use an 8-inch embroidery hoop to pull the material tight and make it easy to write on.

Miscellaneous Accessories

You will also need white crew socks and fake jewelry—be prepared to spend at least ten bucks a finger (I usually wear three rings, none of them fake, but we are economizing, so let's say $30), plus a necklace or a simple rope chain. Elvis loved jewelry, which he wore a lot of. He also had 14-karat or 18-karat gold necklaces made up with his motto on them—TCB. These went to special friends and associates only—it was a real honor to get one.

Can't stop here—you have to get some Elvis shades! Elvis favored those famous silver-framed, tinted glasses and heavy sunglasses you often see him wearing in pictures. Check out the selection at LensCrafters, and ask about their discount for Elvis impersonators. (They really have one!)

The TCB necklace, sunglasses, and many other items you may find desirable can be ordered through the Elvis Presley Estate catalog, which Graceland will send to you at no charge (800-238-2000). Figure about twenty bucks each for the necklace and shades.

The King's "Takin' Care of Business" Jewelry

TCB—"Takin' Care of Business"—was Elvis' motto for many years. He probably borrowed it from Aretha Franklin's hit 1967 recording of Otis Redding's "RESPECT," although the phrase had been part of black America's language for years.

Elvis had jewelry designed for him, by jewelry maker Lee Ableser of Los Angeles, that incorporated an abbreviation of the phrase: TCB. This acronym was mounted above a lightning bolt figure (because Elvis liked to take care of business in a flash, lightning fast! He was a person of very little—if any—patience). The lightning bolt was at least partly inspired by Elvis' lifelong love of a comic-book hero, Captain Marvel. This character turned into a superhero when he yelled "Shazam!" and he was Elvis' guy! The curl on his forehead, the costume with the cape, the love of his country, and so on—everything about Captain Marvel appealed to Elvis. Captain Marvel deeply affected the young Elvis, and Elvis was fond of him right up to the end.

If Elvis' initials weren't monogrammed on his clothing, then TCB usually was. It's said that Elvis thought so much of the phrase that he was even buried with a TCB ring on his finger.

Elvis even named his show band, the one that was with him from 1969 to his death, the TCB Band. (Music trivia fans, take note: this amazing band featured James Burton, the Louisiana guitarist who has also played with the likes of Ricky Nelson, the Everly Brothers, Dale Hawkins, Roy Orbison, John Denver, and Emmylou Harris. Also, the TCB Band backup singers, the Sweet Inspirations, were led by Cissy Houston—Whitney Houston's mom.)

And these are just the essentials—you can do a lot more if you wish. By now you're probably starting to understand that—even if you've done a lot of your shopping at a discount store—being Elvis isn't cheap!

Here's a *very* rough estimate of what it'll cost for costuming basics:*

Pattern	$10
Material and thread	$50
Studs, beads, other accoutrements	$20
Shoes (rental)	$6
Embroidery hoop	$3
Hemmer foot**	$3
Scarf material and thread	$5
White crew socks	$1
Rings (three)	$30
Elvis necklace and shades	$40
Quick-drying metallic marker	$3
Estimated Total	**$170**

OK. When you've got your outfit together to your satisfaction, it's time to move on—and get your act together!

* This is a *minimum* materials cost, and it doesn't include the cost of 40+ hours of labor.

** A hemmer foot is a sewing tool that folds material. This makes it much easier to put the hem into scarves, and will save you a lot of time.

The Sunglasses

Elvis didn't wear those sunglasses just to look cool (though he did look cool enough). He really needed them to protect his baby-blue eyes from bright light. Elvis had glaucoma, the same disease that caused Ray Charles to go blind when he was seven. When he didn't wear his sunglasses on stage, he wore brown contacts to protect his eyes.

Elvis even managed to turn his sunglasses into part of his image. He had his optician, Dennis Roberts, create more than 400 pairs of sunglasses for him. Elvis' collection was valued at $60,000!

Be Elvis!

CHAPTER FOUR

Getting Your

Show Ready

to Go, Man, Go

There are lots of tricks, ideas, approaches, and techniques to mounting a really good Elvis show. Part of it is straight study: it's necessary to delve deeply into subjects such as Elvis' singing style, his onstage mannerisms, behavior patterns, ways of relating to the public, and even his personality.

The other big step is more tangible: getting together a collection of basic equipment and planning the rough outline of your show. (The next chapter will go into the details of structuring this rough outline.)

I can't stress the importance of study to get Elvis down accurately. Don't be discouraged if you never had a chance to see him in person; I don't think that's necessary at all. Remember, the bulk of your audiences will never have seen him in person either; like you, they'll be familiar only with the films and the records.

I'll show you how unnecessary it is to have seen him in person: back in 1989, in Chicago at the Elvis Impersonators International Convention, I was backstage with about thirty or thirty-five fellow impersonators, waiting to perform the finale of our showcase. I asked the group: "How many of you guys ever saw Elvis live in concert?" Much to my surprise, only a few had! I couldn't believe it! These were impersonators who really had Elvis down well, but they'd never seen him live.

Still, it's important to study, because the more you study, the better you'll be. Every step you take to understand Elvis and his style, if done with sincerity and soul, will put you on the right road. So here are a few of the important basics of showmanship, Elvis-style.

I. Basic Singing, Style, and Stage Presence

Elvis' Singing Style

A whole book could be written about Elvis' singing style, but let's stick to just one or two things here.

One important element—important to Elvis' style, his music, and himself as a person—is that he was a mix of all different things. Remember, his first single for Sun Records was a two-sided hit. One song was the bluesy "That's All Right (Mama)," written and originally performed by a black blues singer, Big Arthur Crudup; the other was a rocking version of a country waltz, "Blue Moon of Kentucky," written and originally performed by a white bluegrass star, Bill Monroe. It was this blend of white and black music that made Elvis such a powerful performer.

Elvis came by this mix of music honestly. His years living in the low-income housing developments in Memphis, and before that in a shotgun shack in Tupelo, Mississippi, exposed him from an early age to a rich history of music and culture which continued to inspire him later in life.

His family went to the Pentecostal church, where he heard white gospel singers like Jake Hess and James Blackwood, the inspiration for Elvis' backup gospel quartet. Elvis loved gospel all his life. In fact, he used to sing it for hours in the studio, to warm up before a recording session. It put him at ease.

Elvis' singing style combined elements of black and white music, reflecting the influences of his Mississippi childhood.

Elvis' Teachers

Elvis seriously admired Roy Orbison's uncanny voice. After Elvis' death, Orbison repaid the compliment with a half-time tribute at the 1977 Liberty Bowl in Memphis. It was a very moving presentation: Orbison sang to a spotlit empty chair that held one of Elvis' costumes and one of his guitars.

Sometimes Elvis repaid his debt to black music publicly and sometimes quietly. One example of the latter concerned Jackie "Mr. Excitement" Wilson, whose vocals and dance steps were a major influence on Elvis' stage presence. When Wilson suffered a stroke onstage at age forty-four in the mid-seventies, Elvis arranged to pay all the singer's medical bills.

Elvis also borrowed heavily from Dean Martin's laid-back style, and he was classically inclined as well, trying to incorporate the stylings of forties opera singer Mario Lanza. He also loved country music, and he was a devoted fan of country radio shows like the "Grand Ol' Opry." In particular, Elvis so admired Roy Orbison's four-octave singing voice that he was once quoted as saying that if he could sing like anyone, he would choose Roy Orbison.

But Elvis was also exposed to a rich stew of black music: black gospel, rhythm and blues, and blues. Memphis was—and still is—a hotbed for these styles, and as a teenager Elvis listened to lots and lots of these. Elvis was very aware that he'd borrowed heavily from black music, and he frequently acknowledged it publicly.

Elvis was influenced by many musical styles, including opera, country, gospel, and blues.

An Elvis plastic guitar was made in the fifties, complete with tasteful alligator-pattern case made of cardboard.

Now for Your Own Singing...

The first step in learning how to sing like Elvis may seem obvious, but it's worth saying out loud: learn how to sing! That is, learn how to sing like yourself. Not how to sing like Elvis, just how to sing, period. Remember, you are an individual, not an Elvis clone.

If possible, find a singing teacher you like and trust. He or she will teach you all kinds of techniques, such as those for breath and tone control, and exercises, such as warming up for about half an hour before a show by practicing scales and other exercises to limber up your voice.

If you can't afford formal lessons, there are other ways to learn. Going to a karaoke club, for instance, is an inexpensive way to practice singing in front of an audience—it'll give you experience in using a microphone, standing on stage, developing a stage presence and a rapport with an audience, and so on. Karaoke audiences are usually very forgiving and will applaud a sincere effort.

Don't try singing like Elvis until you've mastered basic singing skills. There are many lousy Elvis impersonators out there and the public is sick of seeing them, so do everybody a favor and wait 'til you're ready. It might take six months if you go to karaoke clubs two or three times a week, a year if you go less frequently.

The next step, of course, is to learn to sing like Elvis. Here I have just one word—study! Watch videos of him singing and speaking, both on and off stage; watch his movie documentaries; watch the concert footage. (Also look for bootlegs, home movie footage, and outtakes from Elvis' career.) Study, study, study!

Karaoke clubs are great places to practice singing in front of a live audience.

When you're first learning to sing like Elvis, one thing to remember is to stay as close to the arrangement as possible—don't improvise too much. Pay close attention to the way Elvis phrased songs. Maybe the most important part of singing like Elvis, in fact, is the phrasing.

At the same time, you have to remember what I said

earlier—that you're an individual. Do you want to slavishly imitate exactly what another singer did, or do you want to put your own spin on it? Find a balance between these two ends—perfect imitation and individual creativity. It'll be hard to do, but it'll be rewarding.

It's easy to parody or make fun of Elvis' voice—but trust me, it's a lot tougher to *really* sing like he did, not parodying it but trying to get to the *heart* of his style. When I'm on stage, what makes me feel right—way more than my jumpsuit looking good or the band sounding good—is when I can think about a song that I'm singing in terms of how Elvis approached it. I think, "What was it about this song that Elvis was able to capture? What emotion?" If I'm lucky, then I get it, really *get* it. And if I really get it, then the audience gets it too. It's kind of magic!

Commemorating the Finger Wiggle

One of Elvis' best-known early performances nearly didn't occur, because of what people perceived as his wild stage movements. The show happened to be at the Florida Theater in my hometown, Jacksonville, Florida. In August 1956, a local judge, Judge Marion Gooding, was determined there would not be a repeat of an Elvis performance there the previous year—a show that had led to thousands of teenagers, male and female, going crazy and nearly ripping off the singer's clothes.

Elvis told reporters, "I can't figure out what I'm doing wrong. I know my mother approves of what I'm doing." But on this second go-round, Judge Gooding prepared a warrant charging Elvis with impairing the morals of minors. The judge threatened to arrest Elvis if he acted in a way that "put obscenity and vulgarity in front of our children."

Luckily they reached a compromise, and Elvis agreed to tone his performance down. It didn't much matter. All Elvis had to do was make tiny little movements, and everybody went crazy anyway. He told a girlfriend later, "Baby, you should have been there. Every time D.J. did his thing on the drums, I wiggled my finger, and the girls went wild. I never heard screams like that in my life."

On the tape of his '68 *Comeback Special*, you can see Elvis joking about the time all he had to do was wiggle his little finger.

By the way, a favorite moment in my own career came at the same theater, forty years to the day after that "wiggling finger" show. I was part of a special program commemorating this anniversary. It was too cool! I got ready in the same dressing room Elvis had used; I gave away prizes, like Graceland wine and trips to Memphis; and I interviewed several people who had actually been there and were sitting in the same seats they'd sat in in '56—some even still had their original ticket stubs and souvenirs.

My show consisted of many old standards that I rarely do, and I was followed by a showing of *Jailhouse Rock*. A great night. And, no, Judge Gooding wasn't there.

Watching Live Shows

I strongly suggest you go to as many live shows as you can. Don't just study Elvis videos! Watch as many performers as you can, both Elvis impersonators and others. I like watching other Elvis impersonators, because I can always pick up things—you look at somebody and think, "I used to do that," or, "That's a good one I never thought of doing—I ought to try it." You're never so good that you can't learn something new.

When you go watch a performer, any performer, look carefully at what is going on *around* the entertainer, not just what the entertainer is doing. Watch how the members of his band and his support team operate. Watch how the lights are used for effect. Pay attention to the pacing—fast song versus slow song; quiet, intimate song versus big, powerful production number. At the same time, remember you'll never truly get better by mere imitation.

Videos as Learning Tools

Two excellent study tools are Elvis' 1968 *Comeback Special* video and the *Lost Performances* video. You get to see a relaxed and raw, unscripted Elvis talking, performing, rehearsing, explaining, and in essence teaching us how he acted and moved. You also get a feel for where he's going with his thoughts and music, and how he approaches his arrangements (which was his specialty—putting his individual signature on a song).

As the years pass, there will be fewer and fewer people who actually saw Elvis perform or who knew him personally, and therefore the accuracy of the Elvis impersonator's portrayal will diminish. (For me, a good Elvis impersonation is performed with the right balance of serious intent and humor. But even a bad impersonator makes you wish, for a different reason but all the more, that Elvis was still with us!) Elvis was a complex and multifaceted individual, and it's inevitable that we'll lose a degree of depth as to what it was all about as time goes on. Luckily, there's quite a bit of video material to educate us.

Obviously, watching all the documentaries and other available videos is the single most easily available way to study Elvis' performance techniques. But if you're lucky, you can get even more insight from bootleg videos—mostly outtakes of the commercially available videos or homemade movies by people who sneaked equipment into concerts. These are really useful, though they're hard to find. Regarding his performance style, I know most of what I know about Elvis from bootleg videos—much more than from the commercially available stuff.

As for seeing one of these yourself, you have to get lucky. I acquired most of mine before Graceland really went after these illegal videos; now they're extremely hard to find. The Presley Estate can be very tough about it—they've got their copyright on Elvis' image, and they're aggressive about policing it. They're not going to do anything if you have a video you recorded yourself—but as soon as you try to sell it or exhibit it, they're not only going to take it from you, they're going to prosecute you.

Elvis' Attention-Holding Tricks

Elvis had lots of little tricks up his sleeve for holding an audience's attention. One of his most dramatic was this: at the end of a song, midway through the show, he would dramatically take off his guitar and move it around as if he were conducting the band, then hurl it over his head and twenty feet across the stage without even looking— and Charlie Hodge, Elvis' longtime friend and band director, would catch it! Charlie always said that never once in nine years did he drop it.

Sometimes Elvis would be so *into* a song—and sense the audience was so into it—that when he ended it he would teasingly ask the audience, "You wanna hear that again?" and immediately do the ending again, picking it up from the tag (the last verse or the last few lines of the song).

Elvis would usually do this on specific songs, like that great old country song "I Can't Stop Loving You." For instance, he would sing its last line, "In dreams of yester, yester, yester, whoa…" Everything would stop then. The drums would be pounding, *Boom! Boom! Boom!* Everyone would be on the edge of their seat waiting, and at precisely the right moment, Elvis would come back with "Yesterday, yesterday…" and again, nothing but *boom! boom! boom!* Sometimes Elvis would tease the audience like this with a false ending two, three, even four times.

This technique is often used by Elvis impersonators, but I would strongly suggest that you do it only *once* in a show, and that it be spontaneous. Since it should never be planned ahead of time (it will sound too stilted otherwise), it can obviously only be done with a live band, not with prerecorded soundtracks.

Another trick Elvis used was what could be called "the anticipation factor." This was a device for building excitement by teasing the audience with an unexpected version of a song they're all expecting. For example, Elvis might start the song "Hound Dog" in a low key and sing it very slowly. This would throw his fans off. Then after a couple of verses, when the crowd least expected it, he would "jump on it"—singing it in its original fast tempo and in the key everyone remembered. He'd have fun with songs, and change things just a little so they stayed fresh.

The only product endorsement Elvis ever made was an early-fifties radio jingle for Southern Maid Doughnuts.

Controlling the Jerks

Sometimes it's necessary to control or disarm hecklers who are trying to ruin your show. The best technique I know of for this is simply to stop singing and look seriously at them. Don't look mean, just stare and stare. Everybody in the place is going to turn and look, and that heckler's going to dry up. Then you can continue with your show—but it's important not to acknowledge the heckler again.

Sometimes people will be talking and not paying attention to you. You can get around this by turning the attention to yourself in a nice, indirect way—like walking over to them and schmoozing with them, maybe leaning over and giving the woman a kiss. You don't have to embarrass them, just redirect the attention. One time, my sister was in the audience, and she was talking and not paying attention—so I took off my scarf and popped it at her and said, "Pay attention!" Most of the people in the audience knew she was my sister, and they got a big laugh out of that.

The point is, you have to at all times be aware of your audience and stay focused on keeping them engaged with you. It's important to command attention and respect at all times on stage—but do it without being cocky or arrogant.

This applies to offstage behavior too. Be professional, but be wary of taking yourself too seriously. Sometimes humor can defuse a tense situation. If people come up to me when I'm in costume and say something sarcastic like, "Yeah, you *wish* you were Elvis," I say, "No, frankly, I don't. I like being Rick Marino. I have a wonderful wife and three great kids…plus, I'm alive and he's not!"

In short, you have to take the show seriously—make sure you do a good job, give people what they're paying for, and don't be sloppy or stupid about it. At the same time, you don't want to take yourself too seriously.

Keeping It Fresh

Another important point is this: you have to work hard to keep your show fresh, by adding new songs and dropping old ones from your set.

Whenever I'm at an Elvis convention and I know I've got hard-core Elvis fans in the audience, I try something new. I know that those people will be happy with whatever I do. I can throw something in that I've never done before—something that I suspect I may not be doing too well yet—but I'll still have a receptive audience. (At the same time, I don't want to do something really *bad*, to the point where it's unworthy of putting before people who have paid admission.)

This way, I can judge whether or not the new song works, based on their response. And they'll let me know! Sometimes I get a great response, sometimes not. Sometimes I'll try a song I really love, that I think is going to be a huge hit, and it *bombs*. It may be that it just isn't recognizable enough, so people don't associate it with Elvis. You learn from these experiences, and you don't repeat them.

The important thing to remember here is how crucial it is for you to try new material and add what works. You don't want your show to get repetitious, either for your audience or for yourself. You've got to find new songs that excite you, that you look forward to singing as the night goes on, and that the people who work with you will look forward to. You don't want to bore your band, your audience, your staff, or your emcee...much less yourself.

At the same time, bear in mind that your audience will change over time. When people see you for the first time, they get charged up and tell you how great you are, and boy, you just absorb that—it gives you the inspiration to keep doing it. You'll keep some of these fans for a while, but then the old ones will drop out and new ones will come in. Don't kill yourself trying to keep the same fans, because they come and go. This is healthy; if you've got the same people seeing your show for years and years, the show'll be old hat to them.

It's important to try out new material. Your audience will let you know if it works.

Re-creating Elvis...But Not Exactly

It's important to think about what period of Elvis' career you're portraying, and to plan your look and your whole show accordingly. I mean, it doesn't cut it to be dressed up in a '68 comeback black leather suit and then to sing a song like "Hurt" that Elvis didn't perform until much later in his career.

Find your own creative, individual look within the general style. In my experience, most Elvis impersonators are either one way or the other—either they're totally off base, going off on some variation that's not at all like Elvis really was, or they're too far in the other direction— they're guilty of overkill in trying to re-create a look, trying to do it *exactly* the way Elvis would.

There's only one guy who really gets away with completely re-creating a look. His name is Eddie Miles. He does the '68 special, *exactly* the way Elvis did it, as a theatrical presentation. That's why people come and that's what they're paying to see. He's got Charlie Hodge working with him (Elvis' good buddy and longtime music director), and it's a good show, so Miles gets away with it.

When you decide which period in Elvis' career you're going to portray, be sure to be consistent.

But his show is not what your general Elvis impersonator wants to do—that type of thing wouldn't work at a fair or in a shopping center or nightclub. It works in little theaters, and most Elvis impersonators don't get to do that kind of show.

Unfortunately, a lot of Elvis impersonators do try to re-create him exactly. And that can be a mistake. They don't understand how important it is to use videos or memories of Elvis' shows as *guides*—as something from which you can improvise. You want to stay true to the form. But you want to make it your own, too. You have to get your own personality in it, and do what works for you. Don't try to make a point of being exact, because that's where you can really mess up. It's really a matter of knowing yourself well—and knowing your boundaries.

I have to harp on this: *You ain't Elvis—Elvis was Elvis, and you're you!* Elvis is dead. And you ain't him.

By the way, this applies to your behavior offstage as well. Don't lose yourself in your characterization. Leave it on stage.

The Bridge

An important element of a successful impersonation, beyond simply imitating the singing style, is to understand the man. I and many others may keep Elvis' memory alive, but what makes us effective is that impersonation is a very *personal* thing.

This works two ways: there's a connection between us and Elvis, and between us and the audience.

Impersonators serve as a bridge, in other words, between the audience and Elvis.

Impersonation is a very personal thing. And that applies not only to the performer and the fan but also—of course—to the person being emulated. You can study Elvis' moves and singing and costumes until you've got them down perfectly, but if you haven't made a study of the man, then it's not going to be authentic—it's going to stay shallow. To really do Elvis, you've got to have a deep understanding of the guy himself.

The best way someone who didn't personally know Elvis can get insights into such a complex man may be to read about him. Of all the books about Elvis, those by Jerry Hopkins, Dave Marsh, and Peter Guralnick are among the best.

II. Basic Showmanship

Equipment and Props

Besides studying and working on showmanship, at this stage you also want to start getting equipment and props together. Many places where you'll be performing will have all the sound system you'll need. All you have to do is show up with your backing tapes (or your band, if you've got one) and plug in. Sometimes, though, for instance at a birthday party at someone's house, you'll need to supply more.

    Note: If you possibly can, get somebody else to set up and sound-check equipment for you. It's important that you be rested and ready for your show, and you won't be rested if you're having to fool around with equipment.

Microphone

I recommend using a Shure™ SM-58 microphone with a cord. Believe it or not, they did have wireless microphones in Elvis' day, at least toward the end of his career, but he preferred the security of a wire since it was what he was used to. There are three other good reasons to use a wire: (1) Using a wire is more reliable, and lessens the chance of something going wrong, especially if you're doing a lot of onstage moving; (2) it's easier to hang on to the mike with a cord, and the cord moving around below the microphone gives the illusion of more motion; and (3) frankly, in my opinion, it sounds better.

However, you should go with what you're used to and what makes you comfortable. And you may want to use both. I prefer the cord, but I do use a wireless when I want to move through the crowd during a show.

Note: Elvis used an Electro-Voice™ Dynamic Omni Directional Microphone. However, I've found the Shure SM-58 to be the most durable, dependable, and versatile microphone, as well as the best value. They can usually be found wholesale or used for a very reasonable price. Shure has a new mike out, a digital version of the SM-58 mike, that is significantly better.

While you are at it, you will need a straight mike stand with mike clip. They come in chrome and black; I'd recommend black, because it's less distracting and visible on stage. You can also purchase colored mike cords— which I do to match different outfits. They will make your microphone stand out, which is good. You can order these from Conquest Sound Co. Inc., 26113 S. Ridgeland Ave., Monee, IL 60449.

Elvis' Contradictions

Elvis Presley was a puzzle. He was worldly-wise, but he was innocent. He was sexy, but he was also cuddly as a teddy bear. He was both hip and tacky. He was both a poor boy who'd made good and a tragic lesson in the pitfalls of success. Studying the man to get an insight into his character— a study that will help you be a better impersonator—will teach you a bit more about this fascinating, complex man.

Guitar

You should get an acoustic guitar at a pawnshop or used-guitar/music shop. Try to get one that matches one of Elvis' more familiar guitars, like the black one he often used. In most cases the guitar is only used for a prop, so don't spend a lot of money. A guitar stand will come in handy for storing your piece during the songs when you just want to croon into the mike.

Other Sound Equipment

I'd strongly advise buying sound equipment, rather than renting. Check the want ads and pawnshops for used equipment, because you can get some great deals. If you buy from a pawnshop, you need to make sure you get it in writing that you have a given number of days to try the equipment out and get a refund if there's a problem. Use a credit card if possible, so you can call the credit company in case there are problems.

You might need to put a couple of hundred dollars into rebuilding used equipment, but often it's worth it—you can end up with very nice equipment, like new, for about half-price. Your basic setup will be speakers, monitors (small speakers that point toward you, so you can hear yourself), and a sound board that controls volume and other functions.

This stuff will pay for itself in a very short time. Plus, it's nice to have it at your house to practice with. And remember, you don't have to buy it all at once—you can do it a piece at a time. I bought my speakers first and later the board—it took me six years to assemble a complete sound-and-lighting system.

Another option is to hire a sound person who brings his own equipment. But every time you hire people to do your sound, if they've got to bring all their equipment with them, you can expect to spend a minimum of $75 to $100. And that cuts into your profit.

If you have your own stuff and you're self-contained, especially with smaller jobs, you can do the job much more economically. For instance, you can hire somebody who's not a pro for maybe $25, just to come along and set things up. It's far more cost-effective. If somebody wants you to do a small gig like a birthday party, and they've only got a $200 budget to work with, you don't want to spend half of it on renting somebody's P.A. system, but still you want to be able to do the job. If you have your own little, self-contained system, you can do gigs like that and still make a profit.

If you can afford it, I recommend hiring a professional to run your sound during the evening. Then you'll be guaranteed things sound great! My man Jim Brown has been with me for years, and he makes sure I sound as good as I possibly can.

Often you can talk the buyer—that is, the person who's hired you—into a bigger fee by convincing him of the superior sound. You say, "Well, you do want this to sound good, don't you? For an extra hundred I can get a pro sound guy, and it'll sound really great. Will you split the cost of using him fifty-fifty?" And usually they'll agree.

The Jungle Room

When you listen to songs like "Way Down," "Moody Blue," or "Pledging My Love," imagine Elvis singing them in a room covered with green shag carpet—they were all recorded in Graceland's Jungle Room. Decorated on a late-night shopping spree at Donald's Furniture in Memphis, it was decorated in a Polynesian style that reminded Elvis of Hawaii. Besides the waterfall and tiki-style furniture, there was green shag carpeting. But the green shag carpeting didn't stop at the edge of the floor. It covered the walls, the ceiling—everything. This created very good acoustics, and the Jungle Room was used as a practice room and recording studio. Toward the end of Elvis' career, RCA would just park their equipment truck out back and run wires into the room for recording sessions.

Spotlight

Again, I recommend buying over renting. I rented a spotlight for my show every time for a long while—though I never paid for it out of my pocket, I was always able to pass the expense on to whoever was hiring me. I'd tell them, "Listen, the show is a lot better with a follow spot, and I will pay the guy to run it, if you will rent it."

Then somebody said to me, "You know, Rick, you could've owned this thing by now." I talked to the people I rented my spot from, and they offered it to me for half the usual price, which is about $1,500. I made a counteroffer of $400 cash; they could keep the spot and rent it out, but every time I rented it the money applied to the purchase. So I only had to rent it a handful of times more and I owned it.

Another good aspect of owning—this is true for sound systems as well—is you can pick up some money on the side by renting it to other performers when you aren't using it.

Scarves, Teddy Bears, and More

Elvis started wearing those famous scarves partly just to add color to the one-color outfits he was wearing around 1970. But they were also good for wiping the sweat off his face—when the makeup gets in your eyes, man, does it sting!

I doubt Elvis' decision to give scarves away was planned. Some woman was probably screaming in the audience, "Hey Elvis, give me your scarf!"

and he handed it to her and the next thing you know it's evolved into, "Hey, let's make a bunch of these and give them away."

Elvis also used to throw teddy bears at the audience when he sang "Teddy Bear." He did this mostly in Vegas and Tahoe—rarely on tour. I noticed him doing it on some bootleg film from '69, and I started doing it too. It's an expensive proposition, though.

You don't want to give away a lot of stuff if you're just doing a private party—it's too expensive—but there are other things you can give away. One idea I came up with on my own is to give away candy kisses from a bucket—it works especially well in an intimate situation: "Here's a kiss from the King, baby."

III. Basic Performance Tips

Fasting for the Show

Elvis didn't eat anything before his shows, and I suggest you don't either. I'd go further and recommend not eating at all on the day of a show. An Elvis show is physically demanding. You need every advantage you can get.

Personally, on the day of a show I'll have at most something light, like half a banana or an oatmeal cookie. You might not want to be so strict—getting sick or having a headache isn't good either. But I find that I have a lot

more zip if I eat very lightly. I perform a lot better, plus my stomach is good and flat for the costume.

Eating just before a show can seriously affect your performance—you'll find that your moves aren't as sharp; you'll feel sluggish and lethargic on stage. Also, you need to watch out for your diaphragm, the muscle that pushes air out and lets you sing properly. It'll be restricted, and your breathing will be shorter, if your stomach's full.

If you do eat, I recommend it be at least three hours before the performance. That's a common show-business rule of thumb—when bands are on the road, they typically will do their sound check early, then have a meal a couple of hours before the show.

The good thing about this is that after the show everybody—your bodyguards and band, your fans and family—will want to go eat, so you can have a nice meal with them and not worry about it upsetting your performance.

Protecting a Valuable Asset—Your Voice

One thing all singers, including Elvis impersonators, need to be especially careful about is overusing their voices. Even a beginner just starting out can have trouble with this. Professionals have to be even more vigilant.

Everybody's got their own little trick for protecting the voice. Honey and lemon in hot tea is well known. Another thing I do is eat cough drops like there's no tomorrow. I don't eat them all the time, but as the day of a show nears, I start popping them regularly. If you have recurring throat problems, don't hesitate to see a doctor or a throat specialist.

The Illusion of Movement

The biggest misconception about Elvis' stage style was that he was constantly bumping and grinding. He didn't just move nonstop—though you wouldn't know that from watching a lot of Elvis impersonators who do just that.

A lot of guys will study the movies, like *Elvis on Tour*, and think that's what his show was like. The truth is, there were long periods where Elvis would just stand or walk. He'd shake his leg, wiggle his fingers, give a look or a smile—but, folks, that's not the same as bouncing all over for sixty minutes.

In his early days, Elvis' movements were wilder and more constant; as he got older, his show grew more professional and streamlined, and this changed. He felt his fans were more comfortable with the *suggestion* of a raunchy movement—just hinting at it, then stopping short and leaving the rest to your imagination. (This self-restraint may have a lot to do with the way Elvis was raised, as a polite and respectful Southern boy.)

What can be deceiving is that in the films, during the moments of relative inactivity, the screen will show the audience or something. Then when a part comes up where Elvis is all over the stage, the camera naturally returns to him. This sets up the illusion of constant movement.

Watch *Aloha from Hawaii* to see how much—or, in reality, how little—Elvis moved. It's the whole concert, unedited. It was all an illusion—he teased people, he'd walk up close like he was going to throw a scarf or something, he'd hold it back…and then, when he got into a big production number like "Suspicious Minds," he really *would* let it go!

Your Entourage

Bodyguards will enhance the mystique that you're working to create. Not only is an entourage very cool—it's a big help in a practical way as well.

When I first started out, I was the only performer on stage. I thought, "Well, I don't really want to be onstage by myself—Elvis never was on a stage by himself, he always had people around him!" So I got my own version of the Memphis Mafia, the bodyguards and helpers who always surrounded Elvis. I put a bunch of my buddies, big guys, in Elvis jackets and sunglasses. When I walked on stage I had all these guys with me—up to eight! But I never kept more than four on stage, because I didn't want to get lost among them. They'd stand there like bookends, and, man, it looked cool!

When I do a show these days, I have bodyguards with me all the time, and not just because it looks cool. It's

important to have your own people with you—people who are your confidantes and friends, who look out for you and help you and make sure your show is as good as it can be.

When I'm on stage, for instance, my guys are responsible for making sure I have water. This may not sound like a big deal, but it's important. The first couple of songs are

Recruit your biggest friends to create your own Memphis Mafia.

usually high and fast screamers like "That's all Right, Mama" or "Blue Suede Shoes," and you need water right away; otherwise, your voice'll be crackly for the rest of the show.

Bodyguards can handle other duties, too, such as going out into the room during the show and checking on the sound level.

Also, the person you're doing the show for—the night-club owner, say—can use your team to relay messages while you're on stage: "There's a special person in the audience that needs a scarf," or "It's so-and-so's birthday tonight." Then, when you're getting some water or scarves, he can whisper the message and guide you: "Red dress, that table." You can walk up to the table and know the birthday girl's name, and people think, "Wow!"

The people on your team can let you know if something's wrong, like your scarf is crooked or your belt's on sideways. And sometimes I'll put my arm on one of their shoulders and say something like, "Well, son, here we are, how you feelin'?" Just because it looks cool.

And if you're doing a show without a band, just a track show, it makes the whole production look fuller to have your bodyguards with you—you still have your entourage. It gives you the appearance of being more important than you are.

OK, so you've progressed to studying hard about Elvis, planning your basic act, and getting your basic equipment and entourage together. Next up—creating a dynamite show and actually getting on stage!

Caddys from the King

Elvis had a taste for giving away cars. Early in his career, he bought a pink Cadillac for his mom, even though she couldn't drive. In the last ten years of his life, Elvis owned about 100 cars, but he gave away many more—I've heard he gave away 4,000 cars in his lifetime...and even tour buses!

One time, when Elvis was appearing in Denver, a local TV news anchor reported that Elvis had bought luxury Cadillacs for a number of Denver policemen. (Elvis had great respect for law enforcement officers.) The anchor-man jokingly said on air, "Elvis, where's mine?" Guess what was waiting for him at the station the next day? The way I heard the story, he was handed the keys live on air and told the Caddy was waiting outside— compliments of the King!

Be Elvis!

CHAPTER FIVE

It's Now or

Never—

Getting Your Act

on the Road

You're ready to go on stage, so let's get down to specifics of how to assemble and pace a killer show. The key word here is pace. In running a successful restaurant, it's said that the three most important things are location, location, and location. When performing, you could say that the three most important things are pacing, pacing, and pacing.

One for the Money, Two for the Show— How Elvis Opened His Shows

Elvis and Charlie Hodge (his longtime friend, vocal coach, and show director) were masters at planning and executing a professional, streamlined, satisfying show.

When the houselights went down, you heard the rumble of Elvis' opening music, the theme from the film *2001* (its actual title is Richard Strauss' "Thus Spake Zarathustra"). Then the drums would start thundering and the band would kick in with an exciting vamp…and Elvis would make his entrance.

The band kicked in over the recorded orchestral music, as eight or more huge hanging spotlights (the "Super Trooper Graphite Burning" model) would start swinging in all different directions, as if searching the room for Elvis. When your attention was momentarily distracted from the stage, suddenly all the spotlights would converge there at once and, BOOM, there he would be. Everyone I've spoken to who attended one of his shows had the same reaction at that instant: "Wow, it's really him! I'm in the same room, breathing the same air as the King!"

The first time I saw Elvis in person, in 1973, I was sitting with my friends in the third row. You could cut the anticipation with a knife, it was so thick! When the lights finally went down and the band started playing the *2001* music, a navy blue Mercedes stretch limo backed up on stage with bodyguards all over it. A door flew open, Elvis jumped out, and 10,000 camera flashes went off.

These flashes really added to the drama of the moment. The Colonel had a rule that people in the audience were only allowed to use Instamatic cameras. These had big flashcubes called Majicubes that exploded in a flash of light—much brighter than the flashes used on today's cameras.

As soon as they saw Elvis, fans would start clicking away without stopping for five or six minutes! The effect of all these flashcubes was so overwhelming that Colonel Parker used to say that he had the best light show in the business and it didn't cost him a dime.

Only three rows away from the King himself.

Your Own Killer Entrance

You can't aspire to an entrance like that, at least not at the start of your career. Still, it's important to make the most dynamic entrance you can. It's like the home field advantage in sports—if your entrance is dazzling and self-assured, the audience will unconsciously be caught up and involved in everything you do afterward, pulling for you to succeed.

And anything afterwards is going to be something of an anticlimax—so don't get on stage too soon! Let the excitement build as long as you can. When you do take the stage, use whatever works: flashing lights, arriving aboard a motorcycle or in a limo, getting on stage surrounded by bodyguards. Be creative—come up with your own ideas.

Let's break down your entrance and first song into ten steps to consider:

1. Where is the show going to be? Indoors or outdoors? Local or in another town? In a mall or stadium? Nightclub or church? Different venues require different setups.

2. What kind of crowd is expected? Large or small, older or younger, hard-core Elvis fans or general public, wealthy or middle class? Are they aware that Elvis is the show, or are you going to be a surprise? Gather as much information about the event as possible. Don't be afraid to ask the person who's hired you for ideas or suggestions. Knowing the type of crowd might help you determine, for instance, what outfit you wear.

3. Timing! This is absolutely crucial. You must plan your entrance down to the second. (With the exit, this is not as crucial.) If you start your show with off-timing, you will usually never get in sync with the rest of the performance. Take your time to plan it and get it right.

4. Use a follow spotlight with color gels so you can set moods for each song, and hire someone competent to run it. (The venue may already have lights—check first!) When the music starts, the spotlight operator should swing the light all over the stage and crowd, so the audience wonders: Where is he? What's happening? The second you walk on stage, the light should stop on you and stay with you throughout the entire performance.

Get it right from the beginning. Your entrance will set the mood for your entire performance.

Likewise, make sure your sound system is solid and your sound man is familiar with everything that's going on. The music should always start before anything else, especially your entrance, and continue throughout the opening of the show without interruption. No pauses! It is crucial that you stick with this format. If done properly this will set up momentum that will carry you through the entrance and opening.

5. Consider your transportation. If at all possible, rent a limousine. This is especially effective if you're appearing outdoors or in a mall. Drive it right down the middle of the mall, through the crowd, if you can! If the show is indoors, you can park the limousine in front of the venue for effect—this looks great and will draw the attention of everyone walking or driving by.

If you're doing the show in a club, meeting hall, or arena, try driving right up to the stage on a Harley-Davidson! (Elvis loved Harleys.) With the music blasting and lights flashing, go right up a ramp onto the stage. If you can't drive a motorcycle, put an "Elvis in Concert" jacket on one of your bodyguards and have him drive you. This works fine, plus he can drive away and you don't have the worry of parking or getting the bike off the stage.

Keep it simple, though. Your priority is getting to the microphone with as few distractions as possible.

6. "Smoke" is always a super effect. There are several ways of producing artificial smoke. Oil makes everything greasy, and it's dangerous if you don't know how to work with it. There's also the kind they use at Disney that smells like chocolate with a chemical base, but it lingers too long and can make everything look smoky through most of your show if the venue is not well ventilated. Dry ice is far and away the best way to go, indoors— but not outdoors, because it loses density too fast outside. Dry ice is kind of expensive—$40 or more to give you the effect you want—but it might be worth it. To find it, check out a theatrical shop or theater. Usually you can rent a dry-ice distributor for another $30 or $40. Allow about four hours to properly heat the water for maximum density and another hour or so for the dry ice to produce fog, then switch on the fan when the music starts. (A black light usually adds a wonderful effect.) Dry ice is great because the fog stays low, it leaves no residue or odor, and it quickly disappears.

7. Think about coming on stage with other people around you. Making your entrance with a large group of people is always exciting—maybe a couple of girls on each arm! Or the bodyguards I talked about earlier.

8. Create pandemonium! Have yourself a few screamers strategically placed throughout the crowd. It's contagious and will get the audience going. (Frank Sinatra used to do this early in his career, though to give Frank credit he didn't have to do it for long. He created a tradition that has continued with Elvis, the Beatles, and every idol since.) When making your first appearance, have a few of the screamers rush you—but don't overdo it. If you're coming through the crowd on foot, shake a few hands—remembering to move quickly toward the stage at the same time.

9. Act professionally, and make sure your people know this is serious business. When you hit the stage, those around you should quickly disperse to their respective positions and assume the duties they are assigned while the performance is going on. Greet the band, grab your guitar, take your time, get your thoughts together—then turn and smile

Plant a few screamers in the audience to help get the crowd excited.

at the crowd, nodding your head as if to say, "I am Elvis…and you are my audience!" Then go straight to the microphone and sing your heart out.

10. Here's a really dramatic trick Elvis used to do when the first song was over—I saw him do this the first time I ever saw him live, and I've never forgotten it. Push your guitar out in front of you, remove it quickly and without looking, and throw it behind you across the stage to one of your more sure-handed guys, who's been strategically placed to catch it. What makes the trick cool is to never, I mean never, look back to see if he's caught it.

Before-Show Jitters

While considering the specifics of your opening, it's also important to think about those crucial moments prior to your show's kickoff. Planning for these ahead of time will give you a big head start on presenting a smooth and professional show.

You're going to have a lot of worries before you go on stage. Foremost in your mind will probably be concerns about the crowd: How big is it? Are they listless and preoccupied, or enthusiastic and pumped? Are there special people out there, such as the press or special family members, who you ought to know about?

Probably second in priority is your appearance. How's the hair, the makeup, and the jewelry? Most importantly, have you forgotten something? (One of my worst blunders happened during the first song of a set. I was really into it—really feeling the music, like when an athlete says he's "in the zone." But I looked down and realized I'd forgotten my belt—an integral part of any Elvis impersonator's outfit. I had to leave the stage mid-song to get it, and it really affected the flow of the show.)

There are a million other details that should always be checked before the show—and remember, it's your show, so you have the ultimate responsibility to ensure that things run smoothly.

One important thing to check is that your onstage power supply is rigged so that you don't overload a circuit. This can lead to the ultimate disaster—one which I was once unfortunate enough to have. I was at a bash celebrating what would have been Elvis' fifty-fourth birthday. It was a huge show, and the crowd was overflowing with press.

I had launched into "An American Trilogy" for the grand finale, when right at the most climactic part of the song, *boom*! The power went out and there I was standing onstage in pitch blackness with no sound. Believe me, I have never felt as alone as I did during those moments before the power was restored. So check those circuits!

To monitor this and other necessary points, I advise you to always write up a sheet, a master checklist, to use as a reference by yourself and everyone who works with you. This will help keep everything straight and minimize confusion. The sheet should include:

- which staffers will be helping you
- which duties fall to which helpers
- who's controlling the guest list
- an equipment list and details of who's bringing what equipment
- a timetable (approximate of course) of what will be happening when: raffles, dance contests, show, picture-taking, etc.
- the set-list of tunes you'll perform.

Checklist

Sound: Jim Brown
Spotlight: Doug Hodge
Props: Barbara Gaither

Song List: Seesee Rider
Burnin' Love
The Wonder of You
And I Love You So
Surrender
It's now or never
All Shook Up

Break For Dance Contest
Teddy Bear
Are you lonesome tonight?
Polk Salad Annie
Love Me
Loving You
Always on my Mind
American Trilogy
Can't Help Falling in Love with You

Taped Backup or Live Band?

Which to use for your backup—a live band or prerecorded tracks? You can go either way; each has its advantages and its pitfalls.

Tape is obviously cheaper and in some ways more versatile—you can have a full orchestra playing behind you on a tape, which you can't with a rock-and-roll band. It's also generally easier—you don't get attitude from a cassette tape the way you can from a temperamental musician! Unless you're already working with a band, chances are you'll choose tape at the beginning.

On the other hand, nothing beats the excitement of a live band. With a band, you'll expand the range of places you can play—while some places can't accommodate or don't want to pay for a whole band, others won't settle for one guy and a tape machine.

With a live band you also can be more spontaneous—you're not locked into following the sequence and timing of the songs on the tape. When you've only got tracks, you're not leading the band. The tracks lead you—you're at their mercy. And if you have a band, you can kid around with the musicians, which you can't do when you're up there all alone (unless you've got bodyguards).

Onstage Disasters

Maybe it's kind of a rite of passage for any Elvis impersonator that some onstage calamity happens at least once. But it may lift your heart to know that even the King had some awkward onstage moments.

For instance, Elvis was known to have ripped the seat out of his pants on many occasions. He always found a way to incorporate it into the show, though, and keep the momentum going and the crowd entertained. He'd laugh and say, "Ha, I just busted the seat out of my pants!" Then he'd tuck a towel into the back and keep carrying on. One time he changed right on stage, with only his band between him and the audience, and he kept on singing. This problem with ripped clothes was why he ended up switching to jumpsuits, which gave him extra room to maneuver.

Tips for a Track Act

You should plan your set to last about forty-five minutes. This will vary depending on the particular gig, of course, but forty-five minutes is a good, standard length for a typical show.

One of the reasons I recommend forty-five minutes is obvious—it's one side of a standard ninety-minute cassette. You want to stick to one side because it gives you enough room—about fourteen songs' worth—and because asking your sound guy to turn the tape over is inviting technical trouble. When you put a track-act together, make a quality tape from prerecorded, music-only CDs or tapes. These are commercially available items, licensed by Graceland, that are designed especially for this purpose. You can mail-order these from King Tracks™ and other vendors.

Always use a fresh tape to ensure high quality. The idea is to assemble a complete show on one tape from start to finish, eliminating any chance of human error during your performance. Let this be the ONLY tape you need for your show. Keep it simple.

If you want to do a longer show (or just want the best quality)

you can always go to reel-to-reel or DAT (digital audiotape) format. But in all the years I've been doing this, I've never needed to go this way. It may be that the buyer or venue hiring you specifically requests reel-to-reel or DAT. If so, this is your chance to go to a recording studio to have it done professionally at someone else's expense. You will then have a studio-quality product available if needed. For the most part, though, cassettes are simple, inexpensive, reliable, and satisfactory in quality.

As a precaution, make a duplicate tape and run it simultaneously with your master on another tape deck. Always have this backup ready in case of disaster! Your audience paid good money, and you owe them a fool-proof show.

Tracks are the only way to go for many private functions such as birthdays, conventions, Christmas parties, and corporate events, where a live band would be impractical. You can cover most occasions if you prepare a couple of different six-song, twenty-minute sets and a couple of ten-song, thirty-minute sets. (You can follow the format below and shorten it a little.) This way, you're always prepared; if whoever hired you has a last-minute change of mind, you can easily lengthen or shorten your presentation.

It's a good idea to always have handy a couple of short, three-song or four-song tapes as well, for birthday parties and other small functions. An example of a good three-song set might be: "The Wonder of You," "One Night with You," and "My Way"—a crowd-pleasing opener, a raunchy middle song, and a big closer. Follow this basic formula using your own song selection, and you will never leave your audience disappointed—guaranteed!

IMPORTANT

If you read the packaging on prerecorded music-only CDs, you will find that when you purchase them, you are also buying the license to use the tracks and sing the songs however you wish (which is why they are more expensive than you'd expect—about $15 for four songs on a cassette or $26 for eight on a CD). To avoid problems, always have all your original licensed CDs and cassettes with you. You have to have these original master tapes in your possession to legally use them (or dubbed versions of them) in your show.

Creating a Set That's All Killer, No Filler

What songs should you play, and when? The pace of a show is crucial, whether you're working with a live band or using prerecorded tapes. You can have a great opening, but you've got to follow it with a tight and exciting set for your show to be a success.

I recommend starting with a fast song, then shifting into a slower one. Next up should be a song that gets the crowd involved—that is, jumping up and down with excitement, running down to the stage, and in general getting wild and focusing exclusively on you.

One of Elvis' favorite tactics for engaging the crowd in this way was to throw stuffed bears while singing "Teddy Bear." Better known and less expensive was his habit of tossing scarves into the audience. Elvis usually chose to do this during certain songs, especially "Love Me," "Teddy Bear/Don't Be Cruel," "Love Me Tender," "Jailhouse Rock," "Hound Dog," and "(Can't Help) Falling in Love," though occasionally he would toss one out at other times during a performance.

When choosing which songs are best for giving out scarves, the speed of the song isn't what's important. What does matter is that your "scarf songs" are placed at intervals throughout the show to maintain audience involvement. Interacting with his fans like this is what Elvis loved to do most of all, and doing it yourself will definitely enhance your experience as an Elvis impersonator.

The rest of your set should be composed of alternating slow songs, fast numbers, and big, showy production songs that bring the house down. Caution: You don't want too many of these last kind, or the whole show will overall seem overblown. Use them sparingly for best effect. You can duplicate a typical Elvis playlist if you like, but you should also feel free to be creative according to your own wishes.

Alternate slow songs with faster, showier numbers.

Different Songs, Different Moods

Songs like "Lord, You Gave Me a Mountain," "Burning Love," "Polk Salad Annie," "Suspicious Minds," "The Impossible Dream," and, of course, "An American Trilogy" are all production songs. Production songs are songs that have a bigger and fuller sound, requiring the full treatment: full band, lots of backup vocals, and dramatic instrumentation and presentation. Sometimes production songs are choreographed for dramatic movement and a big finish.

The key to success with a production song is its placement during a performance—these are bold songs that can make or break the flow of continuity of the show. That's why I recommend using them sparingly.

Besides production songs, another basic type of song is the title song—that is, hit songs from Elvis' movies such as "Love Me Tender." Any well-planned set should include at least one song that "covers the movies."

A third type of song, of course, is your basic rocker—something to get the audience moving. Many of the best of these are the songs that first made Elvis famous: "That's All Right, Mama," "Hound Dog," and "Blue Suede Shoes" are just three examples.

And a fourth type is the slow, romantic ballad—just right for creating an intimate mood. Again, there's no shortage of these from which to choose, although almost any Elvis show would be incomplete without his traditional closer, the gorgeous "Can't Help Falling in Love with You."

Use the big production songs sparingly in your act.

There was an Elvis Presley board game marketed briefly in 1957. By answering true/false questions about Elvis, such as "Elvis is afraid to go up in a plane," players could advance through five levels: Getting to Know Him, Learning to Like Him, Can't Do Without Him, Let's Go Steady, and Get the Preacher.

A Typical "Late Elvis" Track Show

The kinds of songs you choose for a set will depend not only on the period, as in the samples already given, but also on whether you're using tapes or a live band. For a typical track show, make a big entrance with the *2001* music and lead right to…

1. "See See Rider"—the version recorded live
   Sing over Elvis, giving a high-energy beginning to the show.

Now move to a fast song with strong body moves:

2. "Burnin' Love"—the version recorded live
   Keep singing over Elvis' "live" version of this song—Aloha!

Next go to a good "go to crowd" song/ballad:

3. "The Wonder of You"—backing track
   Select a member of the crowd, serenade her, and give her a scarf. Remember that audience involvement!

Next is a slowdown/story song:

4. "And I Love You So"—backing track
   Feel the song and deliver it from the heart.

And now for something different:

5. "Surrender"—backing track

A real crowd pleaser:

6. "It's Now or Never"—backing track
   Go out through the crowd, shake hands,
   get close.

Time for a rockin' oldie:

7. "All Shook Up"—backing track
   Do early Elvis moves—shake it up for them!

Now to give something away:

8. "Teddy Bear"—backing track
   Throw some bears, get the
   audience involved.

**Next, pick a so-called "victim." (Don't
worry, she'll love it!):**

9. "Are You Lonesome Tonight?"—
   backing track
   Sing this to one person directly—
   give her a scarf.

Time to wake up the crowd:

10. "Polk Salad Annie"—the version
    recorded live at Madison Square Garden
    To enhance the energy of your performance,
    sing over Elvis.

Keep the crowd with you:

11. "Love Me"—the version recorded live at
    Madison Square Garden
    Throw scarves, scarves, scarves—continue to build
    the energy.

Now a cover movie/romantic crowd pleaser:

12. "Loving You"—backing track
    Brings back memories—a good song, and
    not overdone and overfamiliar.

Time for a sentimental favorite:

13. "Always on My Mind"—backing track
    I do this for my wife if she's in the audience, and
    the crowd thinks Elvis did too!

And a big production number:

14. "American Trilogy"—backing track
    Big song, very popular, and so Elvis! Put your heart
    into it—usually if it's done well, a standing ovation
    will follow. If you have a cape, use it—fan it out at
    the end of the song. It's a good photo opportunity
    for the audience. Go from here right into your last
    song—no pause. This is extremely important, to
    keep the energy high and constant.

Then the traditional closing number:

15. "(Can't Help) Falling in Love with You"—
    version recorded live at Madison Square Garden
    Make it a big finish and a fast exit.

And into…

16. Closing vamp—exit music
    Tell the sound man not to stop the tape!

Running time: Approximately 45 minutes

A Typical "Late Elvis" Show with a Live Band

Fast entrance (have the band play some suitable riff of your choosing, or use a tape of *2001*).

1. "That's Alright, Mama"
2. "All Shook Up"

Now slow it down...

3. "Are You Lonesome Tonight?"
   Drive them wild—give away a scarf!

Get the crowd involved...

4. "Teddy Bear"/"Don't Be Cruel"
   Engage the audience by tossing a bear into the crowd.

Now slow the pace again...

5. "Baby, Let's Play House"
6. "Heartbreak Hotel"

Faster...

7. "Hound Dog"
   Don't just perform—have fun with the crowd!

Slower…

8. "It's Now or Never"
   A great "cruising song."

Pick up the pace...

9. "Burnin' Love"
   This is a chance for you to use those moves!

Give the band a break:

10. "Love Me Tender"
    Covers a movie song, plus it gives the band a break by using just acoustic guitar accompaniment. And it lets you give away a few more scarves.

Big crowd pleasers:

11. "Hurt"
    One of Elvis' best—take advantage of this super song!

A Late Elvis Playlist

Here's the playlist from Elvis' concert of April 25, 1975, at Veteran's Memorial Coliseum in Jacksonville, Florida. It illustrates well the way Elvis paced his set. (That night, by the way, he wore a beautiful white, two-piece suit with turquoise embroidery on the shoulders and down the side of the outside hem of his pants.)

After his grand entrance, the music segued into:

1. "See See Rider" (fast)
2. "I Got a Woman"/"Amen" (fast/slow and easy)
3. "Love Me Tender" (very slow—Elvis talks to the audience)
4. "If You Love Me"
5. "You Don't Have to Say You Love Me" (big production number)
6. "Big Boss Man" (funky)
7. "It's Midnight"
8. "Burning Love" (churning production number)
9. Band intros/"What'd I Say"/More intros/"School Day" (aka "Hail! Hail! Rock 'n' Roll!") (fast old-time rock and roll)
10. "My Boy"
11. "T-R-O-U-B-L-E"
12. "I'll Remember You"
13. "Let Me Be There"
14. "An American Trilogy" (production number)
15. "Ain't It Funny (How Time Slips Away)" (slow and sad)
16. "(Can't Help) Falling in Love with You" (the traditional closer)
17. And it's into...the exit vamp!

12. "Polk Salad Annie"
Big-time body moves really get the crowd going!

Scarves, scarves...

13. "Love Me"
Really work this song—don't be stingy with the scarves.

Production number coming up...

14. "Lord, You Gave Me a Mountain"
Don't hold back. Use those dramatic Elvis moves you practiced.

Get personal…

15. Introduce the band. Say something about each member.
16. "Welcome to My World"
Go out, shake hands, and treat the audience like they're your best friends.
17. "How Great Thou Art"
A show-stopper—something you do twice in the set.

Another big production song now…

18. "My Way"
Stay focused—you're about to bring it on home!

Closing number:

19. "(Can't Help) Falling in Love with You"
Don't forget to have fun and make this a big finish!
20. Closing vamp (this is your exit music)
Time to make a fast exit as the band plays!

Total running time: Approximately one hour

A Note on Exits

An impressive exit is as important as a big entrance. Elvis always closed with "(Can't Help) Falling in Love with You," and most impersonators do the same. This is not etched in stone, however. "Love Me Tender," "American Trilogy," "If I Can Dream," and "Suspicious Minds" all work well as closing songs.

You might want to borrow the familiar phrase, "Elvis has left the building. Thank you and good night!" which Elvis' emcee, Al Dvorin, always used. You can have your emcee say it after you're gone. (Al Dvorin wasn't kidding. In most cases Elvis slipped out while the band was still playing his closing vamp.)

Elvis' shows typically ran a little under or over one hour, and he never did an encore. As the Colonel said, "Always leave them wanting one more." So leave them begging for more at the end of your set—and don't do an encore. Elvis never did, so why should you?

Be creative with your exit. Try flash pots and smoke for a big finish. Or how about having your bodyguards escorting you out? If you can afford to leave in a rented helicopter, go for it. It's common knowledge among entertainers that what audiences recall best are entrances and exits, so make these memorable.

Go for the big finish: Make your exit as dramatic as your entrance.

Elvis was self-educated and loved to read. Sometimes when he went on tour, he'd take along two trunks filled with books for his dressing room.

Elvis' Entire Evening of Entertainment

Now that you've considered your set list, start thinking about the evening as a whole. Your show should only be one part of an entire evening.

Elvis was a master at building excitement well before he actually hit the stage, creating a whole night's worth of entertainment with him as the centerpiece. You should do the same.

The Elvis experience began with the simple act of buying tickets. This meant first waiting in line for hours, sometimes days, and it was cash-only when you finally got to the ticket window. Elvis had a first-come, first-served policy: if you were first in line, you got front and center seats. He felt his fans deserved what they had waited for, no exceptions.

The day of the show, everyone around you waiting to get in would be so jazzed that the excitement in the air was palpable. Once you finally made it to your seat, you saw all the folks that you'd stood in line with months earlier. You'd pass the time before the lights went down sharing Elvis stories, and then it was show time!

Elvis drew the evening out by providing other forms of entertainment besides himself. He generally had a comedian who opened his shows, warming up the crowd and starting the pace slow and easy. Elvis also liked to give the members of his band space to work out on their own before the main event. He knew that the audience was going to be excited to see him, and anything afterwards was going to be an anticlimax—so he was careful not to get on stage too soon. Instead, he let the excitement build for as long as he could.

Your Whole Evening as Elvis

It's important to plan your appearance so that you are the highlight of a full evening of entertainment. The point is to make the evening an event, and you are the main event. This is especially true if you're doing a track act, where you don't have the built-in excitement of a live band.

The bad news is, this takes more work and consideration than just getting up on stage. The good news is, you can engineer a complete dynamite evening and still do just two sets.

For a typical two-show evening at a nightclub, I recommend a first show of just thirty minutes—a shortened, ten- to twelve-song set—that starts at 8:00 or 9:00. Two hours later, do a full forty-five-minute set.

But there's more to it than that. Say you're in a club, and the doors open at 7:00. People can come in and have a drink or a bite to eat, and you start the show at about 8:00.

During the hour before the show, start running a contest, like a "Shake Like Elvis" dance contest. You'll have maybe three of these during the course of the evening, with the finals at the end of the night. Make sure that the owners of the club are the ones who provide the prizes. These can be prizes that'll bring the winners back to the club—like a $25 bar gift certificate that they can't use that night, so that they've got to come back and use it at a later date.

Elvis Presley lipstick was marketed in 1956 with seven tempting colors: Tender Pink, Love-Ya Fuchsia, Tutti Frutti Red, Cruel Red, Hound Dog Orange, and Heartbreak Pink.

The cardboard to which each lipstick was attached read "Keep me always on your lips" and "Excitingly Alive."

Sets of sixty-six bubble-gum cards relating to Elvis' career were sold in stores in 1956. On one side was a photograph of Elvis. Most cards asked Elvis a specific question such as "Do you get much fan mail?" or "Who is your favorite actor?" (Answer: James Dean)

"Love Me Tender" was the name given to Elvis candy created in 1956.

Your show then runs from 8:00 to 8:45. Afterwards, come out and schmooze with the crowd for half an hour or so. For people who want your picture with them, you've already got somebody there with a Polaroid camera. You can autograph these, sell them for $5 each, and make yourself a little money, since you can usually sell thirty or forty. Schmoozing also involves mingling, meeting people, and doing general PR work ("I'm going to be appearing here or there," "I've done this or that"—you get the picture).

Then take an hour break so you can rest and change. Meanwhile, the second round of the dance contest is happening. At 10:15, you do your second show. After that, do another hour or so of schmoozing.

By then, it's close to midnight—time for the dance contest finals. If you do it this way, you can pretty much keep everyone there till 1:00, and by keeping the crowd there so long you're going to please the club owner—which means you can command the kind of money you want.

Elvis bought clothes from the Landsky Brothers'
clothing shop in Memphis his entire adult life.
The Landsky Brothers also provided the suits for
Elvis' pallbearers.

Be Elvis!

CHAPTER SIX

One for the

Money—

Marketing and

Publicity

Sometimes it's a good idea to think of impersonating Elvis as a hobby. Do it to meet people, go places, and have fun! That way, you'll never run the risk of getting tired of it.

Having said that, I want to talk now about something that's an absolute necessity if you do want to make a dollar or two as Elvis.

Marketing is so important. You've got to have some talent, of course. And you've got to have the costume, the moves, and the rest of it. But the single biggest key to financial success is good marketing. It's the difference between an amateur and a professional who works forty to fifty shows a year (not counting charity shows!) and makes a very decent living at it.

Elvis had Colonel Tom Parker behind him, one of the greatest marketers in the history of entertainment. Elvis deferred 100 percent to the Colonel's ideas about marketing, even when they were crass and short-sighted. (For details of the Colonel's outrageous promotional stunts and campaigns, check out the biographies of Elvis by Jerry Hopkins and Peter Guralnick.) Elvis had tremendous natural talent, but it's very possible he would never have become more than a regional sensation without the Colonel's savvy.

The same thing applies to you. You can be the greatest impersonator in the world, but if you don't know how to get yourself out there in public and negotiate deals and do all the rest of it, then you're not going to go anywhere. One hundred percent of the reason I've been successful as an entertainer—the reason I'm able to do Elvis impersonation as a career—is that I took the time to learn this.

The EPIIA

When putting together your marketing strategy, you should seriously consider joining the world's only professional association of Elvis impersonators. It's a great way to network.

The Elvis Presley Impersonators International Association (EPIIA) was founded by two promoters, Ron and Sandy Bessette, who still serve as its chief executive officers. It has about 300 members and hosts an annual convention in Chicago—a town which boasts about 50 Elvis impersonators. I am proud to be its first and still current president.

The EPIIA brings us impersonators together so we can get to know each other on a personal level. It also lets us see how others approach our shared craft. And it lets us pass on Elvis' legacy en masse to fans, rather than one impersonator at a time. Believe me, the sight of a big group of Elvis impersonators is not soon forgotten—there's nothing like walking into a hotel lobby and finding 150 Elvises in full costume!

The EPIIA also lets us take care of business in other ways. It gives us credibility on a professional level, and awards outstanding individuals with our own versions of the Emmys or Oscars. And it lets us organize benefit showcases that raise money for needy causes in Elvis' name.

For more information, contact me at P.O. Box 16661, Jacksonville, Florida, 32245-6661.

Name That Show!

One of the first things to consider in marketing is an effective name for yourself and/or your show. Often that's the first thing people notice when they hear about you, and you know what they say about the importance of first impressions.

When you search for a title, it's important to consider the legal implications. At first, Graceland tried to put a stop to Elvis impersonators—that is, when they got the rights to Elvis' image and name, they tried to shut us down. They didn't recognize that Elvis impersonators have helped to keep his memory alive all these years. Not to mention all the money they've raised for charity in Elvis' name—a fact I suspect Elvis would be very happy about.

The EPIIA (the Elvis Presley Impersonators International Association, of which I'm president) took Graceland to court over this. The ruling was that a person can do a tribute to Elvis, as long as he's not using Elvis' image or name in a way that can be construed as giving people the impression that you really are Elvis. Doing so would be considered stealing his name or image. Nowadays, Graceland doesn't really care so much, but you still should be respectful and careful when you pick a name.

Don't bill yourself as Elvis. Bill yourself as so-and-so performing a tribute to Elvis. Make this clear in all your material—flyers and tickets and everything else for the marketing and media. For instance, I call my show "Rick Marino's Elvis Extravaganza Show." It's not "Elvis Lives Again!" A wording like that could get you in trouble.

I'd also highly recommend using the word "King" somewhere in your title and publicity material, because nobody owns that. I could've called my show "Rick Marino's Tribute to the King," or something similar. Elvis' name is nowhere in that title, but everybody knows who I'm talking about—and Graceland is happy.

Get a Logo

Elvis had his "TCB" logo—you need one too! A high-quality logo on posters and other material foreshadows a high-quality show.

You could, of course, have a graphic designer put something together for you. But you don't have to spend a lot of money getting a logo designed. Here's one idea: organize a contest where fans submit design entries and you offer a prize to the winner, like dinner with you plus a couple of tickets to your show. In my case, a former fan club vice president designed my logo and presented it to me on the back of a pink-and-black (fan club colors) T-shirt for my birthday! I was touched—I still use it, and always will.

Once you have a logo, make sure that it is exclusively yours. Get the design copyrighted so it can't be used by anyone else. This can save you many headaches in the future. Once you have a nice design, have it made up into letterhead stationery—or you might want to get a rubber stamp of it.

Here's a sample of the letterhead used on one of my own publicity sheets.

Business Cards and Other Basic Promo Material

Along with letterhead stationery, here's more basic promo material you're going to need:

First, some eight-by-ten photos. (These can be mass-produced and you should order lots: you can always sell some at shows and recoup some of your expenses from putting together the press kit.) It's worth it to hire a professional photographer and have these done nicely.

You'll also need a résumé (preferably limited to one or two pages) that includes highlights of your career. If possible, do this on a computer so it can be updated easily. A carefully selected collection of press clippings and other written promo material, such as letters from club owners, will also be needed.

And you'll need business cards. I estimate that business cards alone have generated a third or more of the business I've gotten over the years. Use sharp business cards with your show name and photo on them—and spare no expense! Their quality is seen as mirroring the quality of your show.

Promote yourself right: An investment in high-quality photos and business cards will pay off in the long run.

I know this firsthand. In 1987, I met some photographers who suggested I get elaborate business cards—14-karat gold-leaf printing and a color photograph of myself, printed on very expensive, indestructible developing paper that looked like black onyx. Now you're not going to believe this: for two hundred bucks I got about thirty cards! It did seem self-indulgent, but they were beautiful and unique! I'd been in show business practically my whole life, and I'd never seen anything even close to being so cool.

Well, that night I went to a club in Jacksonville where I usually did three or four shows a year. I saw a friend of mine, and he asked me what I'd been doing lately. I said, "Check this out," and handed him one of the new cards. He had never seen a card like it, and he asked me if I was busy in three weeks. When I asked why, he replied, "I have a new club in Ocala, and I was thinking maybe we could do something."

Now, I know for a fact that it was the card that did it, because he knew what I did for a living before I gave him the card, and he had not even hinted at me doing a show. Anyway, he offered me one of the highest-paying jobs I'd ever had up to that point. The expense of making the cards was money well spent.

Videos as Promotional Tools

My advice about including a video in a press kit is: do it only if real interest and intent is already there, usually after an initial press kit has already been received. This will save you time and expense.

However, videos are the single most effective promotional device you can have, so make sure the ones you send out are entertaining and professional. Producing and copying (dubbing) videos—not to mention mailing them out—are expensive and time-consuming chores, but worth it because videos are so effective.

I strongly recommend buying two VCRs so you can dub tapes yourself. This will more than pay for itself soon enough. If you don't believe me, go spend big bucks to have a videotape commercially dubbed—that should encourage you.

Keep your video presentation as brief as possible. You don't want to show too much, or more than you need to. This keeps interest high. Sometimes less is more! Just five or ten minutes ought to do—give them a taste of your best, remembering to leave your viewers wanting more.

I'd also advise dubbing highlights from your best performances onto one tape, for your own reference in making future tapes. Having the best all on one tape makes dubbing simpler and saves time, and will also save wear and tear on your original master tapes.

Personally, I dislike editing and dubbing tapes for promotion so much that I have no problem sending a postage-paid envelope along with a video I send out, asking for its return when it's no longer needed. In my cover letter to whoever I'm sending it to, I include a note asking for its return. I do, however, invite them to copy it first if they wish.

This procedure usually gets about one-third of my videos back, which is that much less dubbing I have to do. However, I recommend this tactic only with people you think would not take offense. It could easily offend people and cost you work opportunities.

FUJI

Elvis
Extravaganza
Show

The Rick Marino Fan Club
P.O. Box 16661 - Jacksonville,
Florida 32245

904-641-8773

Your Basic Press Kit

Now you've got everything you need for a basic press kit. The basic kit should consist of :

- a business card
- a black-and-white 8" x 10" glossy photo
- a videocassette tape (twenty minutes max), if appropriate
- a résumé (or bio, as it's called in the business)
- a selection of press clippings and other written promo material

All of this (except the video, of course) should fit easily into a folder with pockets, such as a school folder. Often these also have handy spaces for holding your business card. These folders can be custom-made with your photo or logo, though an inexpensive way to achieve the same effect would be to apply stickers with your logo to blank folders.

Don't put too much into your press kit. People don't want to feel overwhelmed. Editors at newspapers or magazines and producers at TV or radio stations are busy people. They want to see information quickly and have it easily available and professionally presented. At the same time, don't hold back out of shyness. It's like writing a résumé for a job—this is one of the few times when you're justified in boasting. In short, send only the best of what you've got—all killer, no filler.

You should constantly be building, refining, and changing your press kit. Figure on putting together and sending out twenty-five or more of them annually.

The Right Price

Deciding on an appearance fee is a complicated problem. You're going to have to figure out two basic things: your own set fee, your normal price for appearing, and a minimum fee, the very least you'll need to make an appearance.

Your set fee will depend on a lot of things, such as the going rate of the competition in your town, your own skill level, the particular venue and length of show, and so on. Look around, ask around to find out what the going rate is, and pitch yourself right about in the middle. It's important not to price yourself out of a possible job or opportunity. At the same time, don't sell yourself short.

Base your minimum fee on the annual average of your costs. Add up office overhead, phone bills, cleaning the costumes, buying scarves, whatever other costs are tied up in costumes and equipment, and the expenses for the rest of the business. Divide into this the average number of shows you do a year, and you'll get a basic break-even cost.

I've figured out, for instance, that it costs me about $75 every time I go out. That's the minimal cost for me just to do a show. So I have to make that amount, at least, even if I do a charity event or something for free. Otherwise pretty soon I'm going to need to stage a charity event for myself.

If a church or other organization asks me to do a benefit, I'm usually happy to do it, but I'll explain that I need $75 to cover my expenses. Such places usually understand that entertainers and artists need to cover expenses to survive. So you shouldn't be afraid to explain that situation to people who want you to do something pro bono, that is, for free. Most places will be prepared to cover your expenses with an honorarium.

If there are commercial companies in your town that hire out entertainers, check out their prices and use them as a gauge to set your own. Remember, you're in competition with them, so think of it this way: the agency is going to charge maybe $200, but they're only paying their talent about $75. I tell people, "Now listen, if you do it with them, you're getting $75 worth of talent and paying $200 for it. Well, why not hire me direct? I'm worth $200!"

Using the Media as It Uses You

Dealing with the media is, of course, a key element in marketing yourself. That's what a good part of your marketing energy and expense will go toward.

Here's a tip on generating media interest when you'd like the media to publicize something—say, an upcoming show:

It's not generally a good idea to call someone cold—that is, without any prior contact. These people, for instance a newspaper's entertainment editor or a TV producer, tend to be very busy, and they get a million people like you calling every day. They may brush you off if you interrupt them. (If you've had prior dealings and know the person, of course, the situation is different, and your call may be welcomed.)

Instead of calling cold, try an indirect approach. Fax them several times anonymously with information about your upcoming event. Next, send (under your own name) a well-presented press kit. Then sit back and wait for them to call.

If you do it this way, you're harnessing the power of Elvis! Elvis is such an interesting character that he's perennially intriguing to the press, year after year. Assume this: everyone loves Elvis, and he's always fascinating. The media especially love him twice a year. They are always looking to get the story—especially the local angle—on Elvis around January 8 (his birthday) and August 16 (the anniversary of his death).

Always be prepared to make yourself available to the media on those dates, but don't give it away. Even when you start out and even more once you're established,

you'll be in a position to barter for publicity. For example, you might make ten pairs of tickets to a show available to listeners of a local oldies station in exchange for advertisement, an interview, or other promotion. You might even be able to work a deal for a live, remote broadcast from your show.

Don't forget: the media need you as much as you need them. Don't be afraid to make requests for what you need to promote yourself. Hey, it's a two-way street! This applies more and more as you make a name for yourself.

When you do get a story or interview, always follow up with a phone call to compliment and thank the people responsible. This will put you in their memory for the future, making it easier to get cooperation when you need it. And you will.

Working the Media

Elvis and the Colonel knew that in interviews things can get misunderstood, misinterpreted, or taken out of context. They were clever when dealing with the media. Elvis spoke very fast, but in his interviews you will notice he chewed every word before spitting it out.

It was also no accident that Elvis held press conferences when fielding questions. One on one, the interviewer is in control and can ask and print what he chooses; but during a press conference, the person being interviewed has much greater control.

Some more tips to remember in interview situations:

• Don't get carried away—be friendly, but brief and to the point. Don't always volunteer more information than necessary. It can make you sound a little desperate.

• Make arrangements to get as much from it as you can, in terms of the deal-making mentioned above, without being arrogant, before the interview.

• Be on time. This sets the tone for the interview. You never get a second chance to make a first impression, so make it count. Put yourself in the interviewer's place and ask yourself what you would want or expect.

• Good manners and consideration go a long way. Elvis knew this, and you'll notice that, even late in his career, he referred to people as "Sir" and "Ma'am" sincerely, which left a memorable impression. Remember, if you're going to be polite, be sincere—anyone can spot a phony or false kindness. You won't win any favorable comments that way. So just be yourself.

Prepare for the Unexpected

You should always be prepared, especially when traveling, for all kinds of unexpected situations—because you never know from day to day what opportunities will arise! This is general advice that can mean a lot for your ability to market yourself by being available on short notice.

I strongly suggest, for instance, that you get a passport and keep it close at hand. You never know when you'll need it quickly.

Case in point: I took my thirty-two-foot limo to Memphis for the fifteenth anniversary of Elvis Week. I had never been to Elvis Week, because I'm always too busy working around that time. This time I went because my fan club president thought it would be a good idea to sell "See Memphis with the King" rides.

When we arrived, there was a message from my wife to call her ASAP. Turned out that an agent in Los Angeles was looking for someone immediately—and I mean immediately—to do a national television show...in Argentina!

As luck would have it, I'd had a funny feeling before leaving home. This was the first time I had ever taken that week off, and something had told me that (even though I wasn't scheduled to perform) I should bring along some things: three costumes, three bodyguard jackets, Elvis glasses, cassette tapes of track shows, and, yes, my passport.

I called the agent, and a deal was made. I sent my limo and driver back to Jacksonville, and at 5:00 a.m. the next morning I was on my way to Argentina! It was a memorable trip: I was interviewed in Spanish on live national television, gave a good performance, and met a lot of wonderful folks, including a popular band called Los Super Ratones that later hired me to produce one of their CDs. The moral is: be prepared! It can mean the difference between missing an engagement and making it happen.

The King Appearing Live in Your Hometown!

Local Elvis history can be very exciting to talk about with the media in your town.

I have always thought of myself as being a representative for Elvis, his memories, and all his fans in my hometown, Jacksonville, Florida. So I've researched Elvis' history here, and I've found it to be a very effective tool when talking to the media.

Reporters love hearing these local stories about Elvis—they gobble them up! Often these reporters are young—they have been in the field for ten years or less, and so haven't covered anything about Elvis themselves. For them, the local angle makes a great story.

So I'd strongly urge you to research whatever connection may exist between Elvis and your town. Find people who have stories of their own and interview them yourself. Go to the local library and see what you can dig up. Not only is this fun—it'll help you in your own career, because you can use those stories in interviews and as onstage patter.

Don't You Play Me for a Fool

It's a constant battle to avoid having the media make fun of you and try to make you into a fool. I don't mind the media poking a little fun, but there needs to be a line, somewhere between having fun and making fun of my chosen profession.

The best advice I have on this score reflects what I said earlier about dealing with hecklers onstage: you have to command attention. The same thing applies to your

On the set of A Honeymoon in Vegas *with star Nicolas Cage.*

dealings with the media. Even when you're off stage, you have to work to command that same respect.

When, say, a TV station wants to do something on you, and you go out of the way for them, and they just want to do some dumb satirical thing—that's an insult and a waste of time. My way of dealing with this is to say something like, "When was the last time you saw anybody do an interview like this straight, without making fun? Don't you think it'd be a better interview?"

There is a place for parody, and it can be hilarious if it's done right. A good example is the movie *Honeymoon in Vegas*, which I was involved in. Because Andrew Bergman, the director, didn't make us real impersonators look like fools, it was amusing but not degrading. I was personally gratified that this was the director's intent, and that he was open to suggestions to make sure it was presented as such.

Contests

Entering an Elvis impersonation contest can be fun; it also offers onstage experience and an opportunity to learn from others. It can also give you a shot at greater exposure as your confidence grows—and a chance to earn some prize money.

Contests have drawbacks, though. For those of us who are fairly well established, they're good opportunities to see friends in the business we might not otherwise get to see. Unfortunately, though, people tend to take the winning and losing pretty seriously, so they don't always want to hang around afterward and chat.

For your own self-esteem, remember that the results of a contest are just the opinions of a few judges on that particular evening or day. In many cases, these people aren't even really qualified to decide such matters, so who they choose as winner may be nothing more than a whim. I have noticed recently that a lot of the bigger Elvis festivals are getting smarter— staging contests with professional, well-known impersonators, and covering their expenses and travel costs. At the same time, these contests still have open invitational for non-pro hopefuls.

The pro contest is usually a one-night presentation, with each of the six to ten contestants performing only two or three songs and competing for three top places. This gives each contestant a 35 to 50 percent chance to be in the money, and this amount is usually sizable enough to attract top entertainers.

You might prefer to treat contests, as I do, simply as a spectator sport. That way, you can just enjoy the show and learn from others. And you're never too good to learn!

Joining an Existing Fan Club

You may find it useful—and fun—to affiliate yourself with one of the many existing Elvis fan clubs. There are lots of reasons to do this, foremost being that Elvis fans will help you like no one else can, short of your mother! They can be a big boost to you, especially early in your career. An already-existing club will often rally around you, promote you, and work diligently for you, and maybe even in time help start up your own fan club. Most of these clubs have their favorite impersonator or two…one might pick you!

There are many kinds of Elvis fan clubs all over the world, and typically they'll have conventions once a year with vendors selling and buying everything Elvis. A special guest or two might be featured—such as someone from Elvis' life, maybe one of his bodyguards, a family member, friend, or a costar from a movie—and nationally known impersonators often perform. So if you're just starting out, attending a convention is a great way to get a look at other impersonators.

These conventions give you the opportunity to meet other fans of Elvis besides yourself. You can buy, sell, or trade memorabilia, network a little, and maybe give yourself an excuse for a weekend trip. Most clubs are nonprofit, furthermore, and will work to raise money in Elvis' name for a designated charity.

Joining a fan club, in short, is a great hobby that doesn't take a lot of time and effort—though it can get expensive if you get carried away by Elvis Fever or the "I've gotta have everything I see!" bug. It's kind of like gambling, so budget yourself and be selective.

The Inspiration for "Heartbreak Hotel"

Songwriter Mae Boren Axton met Elvis at the first in a series of shows he did in the Jacksonville area in 1955. Axton invited Elvis to rest up at her home when his Florida tour was over a few days later. She also promised to write him a number-one hit.

While Axton was waiting for Elvis to join her, a friend of hers, Tommy Darden, stopped by to talk. Darden told her about a newspaper article he had recently read about a man who had committed suicide and left a note reading, "I walk a lonely street." Remembering she had promised to write Elvis a song, Axton was struck by inspiration, and said, "Let's put a heartbreak hotel at the end of his lonely street!"

"Heartbreak Hotel" went on to become Elvis' first national hit and first million-dollar seller—the *Billboard* Number One Song of 1956 with a twenty-seven-week stay on the Top 100 chart.

Personally, I'm affiliated with the Elvis Always fan club in Folkston, Georgia, E.P. Continentals, "The Club that Elvis Named," in Orlando, Florida, and, most recently, Elvis Friends Hollywood in Burbank, California. The latter has a wonderful annual convention on May 1st (Elvis' and Priscilla's anniversary) in Palm Springs, Ca., and the Riviera, which has a rich history with Elvis as the house he used as his honeymoon hideaway.

If you have trouble finding a fan club, there are several books available that list various clubs. Most likely, you'll want to join one in your area. If there isn't one locally, you'll need to search further— or start your own. You want to register with Graceland if you start a new fan club—you don't have to have

their approval, but you're going to go a lot farther. Graceland won't charge you any money or anything, and they'll help you out; they treat the fan clubs very well— especially during Elvis Week in Memphis.

A final word about fans: fans come and go, and sometimes will return and sometimes not. This change is a healthy thing, so don't let it bother you. It's going to happen and there's nothing you can do about it. New fans are great and bring a freshness to your career, while longtime fans are always the most cherished, as well they should be. Fans who have been there the longest sometimes represent a security blanket, especially when you're first getting started, but like anything else, sometimes it's time to move on and grow.

Don't Return to Sender

One of the most important things you can do when marketing yourself is to put together a good mailing list. Your mailing list is the heart of your business. Its strength can make or break you.

Let's say you go to a nightclub and say, "I want to do a show here." Remember that you're a novelty act—you can't go in every week. Your act should only appear once in a while in a given club. Therefore, it's important that you guarantee you can bring people into the club who would not ordinarily come. You need to convince the owner that this is an opportunity to bring in new customers and to have a full house on a slow night.

The size of your mailing list is the heart of this guarantee. A rough rule of thumb is that a mailing list of 500 will guarantee about 200 people who actually turn out. I know, for instance, that wherever I go a minimum of 200 people will show up to see me.

The people coming directly as a result of receiving a mailing from you will spend, say, $10 each to get in to see you. Since you're the reason they're there, you can say to the club owner, "I want $2,000 as a minimum guarantee"—in other words, he's giving you a guarantee of the door. Anything on top of that is gravy for both of you. You can say to the club owner, "Anything over the $2,000 minimum we'll split."

Graceland included a stable to house the horses that belonged to Elvis and Priscilla. Elvis' favorite was a golden palomino quarter horse named Rising Sun. In honor of his horse, he named his barn The House of the Rising Sun. Most of the horses that Elvis kept have died, but you can see their offspring (and the few remaining horses) at Graceland today.

Creating Your Mailing List

There are several methods you can use to get names for your list. The most common and effective is to gather information from people who come see your show. Here are some ways to go about it:

• Ask people in the audience to fill out cards, commenting on your show, that you've left on the tables. (Or ask them to sign a guest registry when they come in the door.) Have them include their names and addresses, and ask for permission to send them information about future shows.

• Hold a raffle. After your emcee announces details of the raffle, you'll get maybe 40 or 50 people responding from an audience of 300. (Try to get the club to buy the prizes.) Ask those who participate to fill out mailing information, and ask for permission to put them on your mailing list. And don't forget that word of mouth is the best form of advertisement—those initial 40 people might come back with friends!

• Ask a fan club to use their mailing list to create your own. But you need to remember that these people are first and foremost Elvis fans—not your fans. So I'd recommend building your fan base initially from the general public, so you don't have to depend on any particular group.

When you do a mailing, it's cheaper to send a postcard than a letter, and if your mailing is big enough, you can do it bulk rate. I periodically send out a four-by-six postcard with schedules and other information. Often you can pass this expense on to the person who's hiring you for the next show, since it's publicizing their place as well and will help guarantee a good turnout.

☆ ELVIS ALWAYS ☆
FAN CLUB
- proudly presents -
The Sixth Annual
EVENING OF ELVIS MEMORIES

Featuring:
Rick Marino
"Mr. Showman Himself"

...plus

A portion of the
benefit N. Flor
Founda
further in

Elvis
Extravaganza
Show

Name _____
Address _____
City_____ State_____ Zip_____
Phone_____
Where did you see the show? _____
COMMENT:

Your Own Fan Club

Eventually what happens, after you've built up a mailing list and have a base of regular fans, is that some of these regulars will start asking you what they can do to help. They're loyal and excited, and they'll be happy if you ask them to do something in the show, even if it's only helping you with the raffle or putting out comment cards.

Sooner or later, one of them will talk to you about starting a fan club up for you. Having your own fan club's a good thing, and I'd recommend it; I've had several over the years, and all of them have done me well. But you've got to have other people do it—you can't do it yourself.

When somebody does want to start one, say, "Great!" (after making sure their intentions are true). Turn your mailing list over to them and be available if they need you. They'll organize picnics and other events, which is cool—just make sure they know you'd like to approve everything before it happens. Otherwise, let them do it all. Don't get involved—it's their deal.

And make sure your fans know it's their fan club— they'll want to work harder and they'll feel better about it, if it's their own creation. Show the fans respect, don't expect anything, and appreciate everything they do. If the fan club is their deal, and you're just there if they need you, it'll be much better.

Making yourself available to the fan club is key. Why do you think the country-music industry has Fanfare in Nashville, when the stars give up a week of their time to come and be with their fans? It puts the stars in a very positive light to be available. It goes back to my point about building a bridge—that bridge between you and the

Crazy Gimmicks

Anybody who ever dealt with Colonel Parker had stories about his genius for crazy marketing schemes. He came from a carnival background, and his philosophy was always to do anything for a buck. In an interview reprinted in Mick Farren's *Elvis in His Own Words*, Elvis recalled:

"One morning I looked out of my bedroom window on the second floor facing the highway, and spotted a man picking up leaves outside the stone fence and stuffing them in a valise.

"I told my manager, Colonel Tom Parker, and he went out to check on things. He asked the man what he was doing with the leaves and the man said he'd got a big thing going up in Buffalo, New York, selling the leaves for souvenirs. He was selling them for $10 apiece.

"The Colonel admired the man's ingenuity so much, he let him go. The fella kept right on picking up leaves— just the choice ones—and putting them in his bag.

"[But] the Colonel got to thinking about the 'leaf gimmick' as he called it, and contacted the local Memphis radio station. He invited them over to come out and rake up 10 or 12,000 leaves and offer them as prizes in various Elvis Presley contests. My discs got a bigger than ever radio play and those leaves went like wildfire."

fans, and you and Elvis. You've got to keep that bridge open so you're accessible.

Do not, however, allow your personal life to mingle with your professional one. It's OK if the fans know everything "Elvis" about you. But be careful to keep your home and family affairs separate.

Colonel Parker could make money from anything if it had Elvis' name or picture on it. At an Elvis show, a fan could buy merchandise ranging in price from 25 cents to $5.

I've found it's always paid to be kind to my fans. When meeting your fans, say, after a show, be patient and attentive. Listen to their stories, especially about the passing of Elvis and how it affected them. Remember, as bizarre as it sounds, you are the closest they'll ever get to meeting their hero. Be agreeable and passive; let them monopolize the conversation. Say very little, but interact positively with them. Accept gifts from fans graciously and with appreciation.

If by chance you happen to engage in a conversation with someone who knew him, avoid touchy subjects like his death. It's painful for them to talk about. I know—I've met many of them, and they all loved the man.

Merchandising

As any fan knows, the Colonel merchandised Elvis relentlessly, and the Presley estate continues to do so. Should you merchandise—that is, sell your own souvenirs? From personal experience, I advise you not to. I've tried selling "Rick Marino's Elvis Extravaganza" T-shirts and posters and so on, but I found it not cost-effective and a lot more trouble than it's worth.

For me the best thing is to get a bunch of eight-by-ten pictures to autograph, or to do the Polaroid thing, where people line up and get their pictures taken with you. The way this works is: you've got somebody there who takes your picture with the fan. Then you put the photos into little sleeves with your logo stamped on them. You can pre-autograph them, but you can also sign them individually—you know, like: "To So-and-so—I just want to be your teddy bear—thanks for coming." I use the profit from these photos to pay for my scarves and my teddy bears, little extras for the fans.

You might find it best to have both eight-by-tens and Polaroids available at the show. People usually would much rather have a photo of themselves with you than an eight-by-ten, but if I'm tired or not in the mood, then I can just give them an autographed eight-by-ten. Sometimes I'll do both—I'll offer the Polaroids between shows and the eight-by-tens after the last show.

Costumes as Marketing

I'm going to harp again on something I said when I was talking earlier about costumes: when you're putting together your outfit, don't cheap out! This is a marketing consideration as much as anything. If you have a $200 costume, you might be worth only $50 to a club owner. If you have a $500 costume, you'll be able to charge $100. After you've done, say, twenty shows, that means you've got $800 ($1,000 minus the initial cost of the costume) versus $1,500 ($2,000 minus the initial cost of the costume). Which would you rather have?

The point is, your success will be directly influenced by how much you put into your costume (and other aspects of the show). A first-rate costume equals a first-rate show in the audience's mind, and the value of you as a commodity goes up as you put more money into your production.

In a lot of ways, it doesn't matter how good you do Elvis—if you're able to put together a nice program and you've got a great-looking outfit and you've got your marketing together, you can command the money. People will think you're better than you are. I know that sounds weird, but it's true, and, as simple as that sounds, it's the secret to success.

Colonel Tom's Campaign

Elvis himself was the product and the focus of the greatest marketing campaign of all time. Colonel Tom Parker, ex-carnival huckster, succeeded in making millions of teens want to be with Elvis all the time and want to be Elvis.

The Colonel and Elvis would have been successes on their own, even if they had never met; together, they were unstoppable. Parker liked to say that when he first saw "his boy," the only thing Elvis had was a million dollars' worth of talent; after they joined forces, Elvis had a million dollars as well.

He was a notoriously tough negotiator; film producer Hal Wallis, who made many Elvis movies, once remarked, "I'd rather try and close a deal with the devil." The Colonel turned down deals that some people thought he was crazy to pass up. He turned down a performance at the White House because the government refused to meet the Colonel's $25,000 fee. He lost the lead in *West Side Story*, *Sweet Bird of Youth*, *The Defiant Ones*, *Thunder Road*, *Midnight Cowboy*, and Streisand's remake of *A Star Is Born* because the Colonel thought each was a bad move. The Colonel even turned down the Queen of England! In '61 Elvis was invited to perform before Queen Elizabeth, but the deal fell through because the Colonel, in America illegally, had no passport and refused to let Elvis play outside the States without him.

Every time I get into costume and psych up for a big show, I say to myself, "I am Elvis!" I become the vessel that keeps Elvis in the present tense. And when I'm in costume, an amazing thing happens: I can do practically anything I want. I can enter a venue without question, cause heads to turn wherever I go, or enjoy a complimentary meal at a nice restaurant.

Probably nothing demonstrates more the extent to which Elvis has become an admired icon than the fact that even his impersonators get treated like royalty. Decades after Elvis "left the building" for the last time, a person can dress up like him, walk into a room, a building, a stadium—even the Olympics—and stop everyone in their tracks. Even if it's only for a minute—just long enough for them to ask, "Hey, is that…Elvis?"

A Defining Moment

People sometimes ask me to define in one story what it's like to be an Elvis impersonator. When they do, I always think of what happened at a Houston Oilers–Miami Dolphins Gator Bowl showdown in 1989.

It just so happened that Oilers owner Bud Adams always left a ticket at will-call—plus a guarantee of one million dollars cash—if Elvis showed up at one of his games! (I've heard that Jerry Glanville, ex-coach of the Oilers and then the Atlanta Falcons, left a pair of tickets for the King at all his home games as well.)

Anyway, I had been approached by a Jacksonville nightclub to appear at the Gator Bowl for promotional considerations, because Jacksonville was trying to get an NFL team. We—me plus a cameraman, limo driver, and bodyguards—managed to purchase six tickets to the sold-out game. The day of the game my gang and I pulled up at the Gator Bowl, totally unannounced, in a big, white, ultrastretch limo. Our presence caused such a sensation that we were given escorts and ushered right on in. We didn't even need those tickets we'd spent more than $200 on.

Elvis Presley is still so beloved that even his impersonators are often treated like royalty.

When we entered the stadium with our entourage of police security, the crowd of 75,000 stood up and went crazy! News cameras were everywhere and complete pandemonium broke out as we walked around the field.

The network covering the game for primetime national television asked if I would do a "bite" for an exit to a commercial; so, surrounded by security personnel and hordes of screaming people, I said to the camera, "Jacksonville and the NFL are definitely a winning combination—take it from the King! Thank you, thank you very much. Uh, by the way, tell Bud Adams I want my million bucks!" And then it was cut to commercial.

As I left, the crowd did the wave for me and hollered "Elvis lives!" The director of the Gator Bowl came up and thanked me, and that sound bite ran all week on ESPN Sports.

And the end of the story? Jacksonville eventually got its own team, the Jaguars, and Houston and Bud Adams lost theirs. Just goes to show, it never hurts to have Elvis on your side.

Wild Days in Vegas and Chicago

Every year at the EPIIA convention, which is normally held in Chicago, it seems like something bizarre happens.

In Vegas in 1994 I was hired to shoot some "tags" (short promotional shots) for the TBS Network, which was planning "Night of 100 Elvises," a marathon showing of movies starring you-know-who. The shoot was a lot of fun and I used the occasion to raise a bunch of money for the EPIIA and a few of my colleagues.

I assembled a diversified group of impersonators from all over the world, to get as wide a variety of styles as possible on camera. For one scene, the director asked us to speak the King's trademark expression simultaneously.

Problem was, the exact words the director asked for were "Thank you

very much." We did several takes, all lousy, and finally I suggested that we use the more accurate "Uh—Thankya, thankya very much." All the guys went, "Yeah, that's it!" And we did it in one take, right on the money. The crowd watching us cracked up. We were all surprised too—but we acted cool, like we'd planned the whole thing.

I also remember what happened at the first EPIIA convention in Chicago in 1989. The big finale showcase featured forty or so of the top impersonators, including myself. It was supposed to be a knockout, and it was—but not in the way we planned. When we went on stage, the risers that were supposed to support us collapsed! All forty of us fell into the crowd—talk about flying Elvises! Fortunately, no one was seriously hurt, but still the crowd jumped to its feet in surprise. It was a hell of a way to get a standing ovation.

Perks

I've enjoyed a lot of nice perks as an Elvis impersonator—otherwise, I'd have to be a millionaire to have done all the things I've done.

I've traveled all over the world, expenses paid. I've gotten tabs at nice restaurants and free tickets at movie theaters for helping out with promotions. The really cool part about the movie tickets was not saving a few bucks but being able to just walk right by the line waiting to buy tickets. I was single then, and talk about impressing a date!

One of my sweetest experiences was completely unexpected. After I got home from my gig in Korea and at the Olympics, I was besieged with calls—the Olympics and Elvis were big news. About two months later, my mother and I were driving home to Jacksonville from Maryland, and in some small town in North Carolina, we stopped at a Pizza Hut to eat. When we asked for our check, the manager said it was on the house. He'd seen me at the Olympics! He gave us a pizza for the road, asked for an autograph, even called his wife and kids to come up and meet me.

Without a doubt, my biggest perk as an Elvis impersonator was meeting my wife, Susie. Her uncle was my manager for a while, and she came to some of my shows. I eventually proposed to her onstage, and, lucky for me, she accepted.

The Movies

You never know where being an Elvis impersonator will take you. *Honeymoon in Vegas* is a great comedy released in 1992, starring Nicolas Cage, Sarah Jessica Parker, and James Caan. Being cast as "The Truck Drivin' Elvis" was a wonderful experience, even if I did end up on the cutting room floor. I was treated royally in Vegas, and got to meet the stars as well as director Andrew Bergman. Nicolas Cage told me, "I'm a major fan of the Big E!"

While shooting my big scene, I got some of the best advice I've ever gotten in my career. I was really nervous, and Mr. Bergman asked, "Rick, is everything all right?" I said, "Well, I'm a little nervous and not being an actor and all I really don't know what to do." He immediately replied, "Rick, are you Elvis?" I said, "No." He said, "Then do what you normally do." I said, "What's that'?" He said, "ACT!!!"

I later had the opportunity to work on another motion picture, *Finding Graceland (1998),* as technical advisor and special consultant. (I called this "having a great time and getting paid for it.") The movie stars Harvey Keitel, with Priscilla Presley as one of the executive producers.

Harvey was fascinated with the technical aspects of impersonation. When he and I met to discuss how to approach his Elvis-inspired character, the first thing he asked me was, "Is being Elvis like method acting?" All I could tell him was my approach: take 50 percent of Elvis and 50 percent of myself and meld them together to create a character or caricature of the King.

Rick Marino and actor Sarah Jessica Parker.

I don't think the hoopla that surrounds Elvis affected Harvey's approach. What did fascinate him were the things that defined Elvis the man. Where did Elvis come from? What were his beginnings, and what were the people from there like? Who was Elvis as an individual?

Harvey was also interested, as he put it, in why Elvis "fell and didn't get up. And how come no one at Graceland addresses this?" In other words, what went wrong at the end of Elvis' life? Harvey felt that this was a very important part of who Elvis was.

On a personal note, Harvey was great to be around. I'm glad that I got to work and hang out with him for nine months. Thank you again, Elvis!

Private Quarters for a Public Man

One thing you won't see on any tour of Graceland is Elvis' private quarters. Even Elvis, a man whose life and death were so public, had to have an escape and a sanctuary that was strictly off-limits to the uninvited. Elvis created this sanctuary in his bathroom.

This retreat was, of course, no ordinary bathroom. The shower is round and in the middle of the room. There is a closet where he kept his extensive wardrobe. But Elvis didn't use his closet just for storing clothes—it also housed a sleeper sofa and a refrigerator, where he kept the goodies he munched on while watching his favorite shows. Also in the bathroom was a huge lounging chair where he often spent time reading.

In the final months of Elvis' life, he often had trouble sleeping, and would escape to the bathroom to read through the night. On August 16, 1977, Elvis did just that. Unable to sleep, he sat down to read in one of the few truly private places in his world. It was there that he died.

Elvis consultant to the stars: Harvey Keitel benefited from an impersonator's expertise.

There are also some very good videos of Elvis performances available, including:

1. *The Great Performances (parts I and 2)* (1990). Each tape is about one hour long, and they are sold separately.

2. *The Lost Performances* (1992). This is an incredible video, with just an amazing story to go with it. Seems these outtakes were forgotten in a warehouse for twenty years.

3. *Elvis '56* (1987): This one began as a Cinemax one-hour TV show.

Television Specials

Two of Elvis' TV specials are available on video, and the third has never been released. It can be found, however, if you are persistent; you should be—it's worth the search.

1. The *'68 Comeback Special* (1968): This is fantastic stuff—Elvis' brilliant return to live performance. It first aired December 3, 1968, and ran ninety minutes. (Another video, *One Night with You*, highlights an extended version of one of the segments featured in the original show.)

2. *Elvis: Aloha from Hawaii* (1973): Another must-see performance. He looked great! Elvis sang twenty-nine songs in a program that lasted an hour and a half. This one was broadcast live via satellite around the world, reaching one and half billion people. It was the biggest audience ever for a single performance. Even though it was filmed live on January 14, it didn't air in the U.S. until April 4.

3. *Elvis in Concert* (1977): CBS-TV special that aired after his death on October 3. Elvis sang fourteen songs in a special that was originally planned to run two hours, but was cut to one hour. Elvis didn't look his best here. He looked heavy and tired, but vocally still was outstanding. The footage was filmed just a month and a half before he passed away. The folks at Graceland chose not to merchandise this concert special. It's a shame, but it isn't impossible to find.

Books

There are dozens and dozens of books on Elvis available, and new ones are constantly being produced (like this one). Some are worthless trash, some are well worth your while (like this one!). Here are some of the best.

Jerry Hopkins. *Elvis.* (New York: Simon & Schuster, 1971.)

A straightforward biography that covers the basic facts of Elvis' life through the late 1960s. The story is continued in Hopkins' *Elvis: The Final Years.* (New York: St. Martin's Press, 1980.)

Peter Guralnick. *Last Train to Memphis: The Rise of Elvis Presley.* (Boston: Little, Brown, 1994.)

Detailed, respectful, and perceptive. Concluded in Guralnick's equally essential *Careless Love: The Unmaking of Elvis Presley.* (Boston: Little, Brown, 1999.) Taken together, this is the most thorough study of Elvis to date.

Custom Outfits

If you've just got to have one of Elvis' late-period, very expensive, very hard-to-make outfits, and if money's no object, you can buy yourself some really nice things. There are several companies that custom-make Elvis outfits and costumes for other performers, such as country-music stars.

One is B&K Enterprises of Indiana, named after its owners, Butch and Kim Polston. B&K pretty much got their start with the first Elvis Impersonators convention, when they were able to network with impersonators from all over; before that they'd just been local, for the fifty or so Elvis impersonators working in the Chicago area. All the Elvis impersonators at the convention already had their homemade costumes, but none of their outfits looked anything like Elvis at all; these outfits were their own creations. Butch had a bunch of suits that he had made, and when all the guys met him, they realized how much better his stuff was. As a result B&K is a hundredfold bigger.

Butch makes costumes not just for Elvis impersonators but also for celebrities in the country-music business and elsewhere. They're great, but I have to admit that they're not top-of-the-line. There are a couple of other companies that make really great costumes—one guy in particular

makes the best suits in the business, using the same materials that Elvis' costumes were made of. He's the Armani of Elvis costumers, but his price tags are astronomical—you won't get a suit from him for less than $3,500!

You can also contact Tandy Leather company for leather goods. Mention Elvis for a discount. For more info on costume suppliers, contact me at P.O. Box 16661, Jacksonville, Florida 32245-6661. We'll get you suited up!

For booking contact:

A Unique Entertainment, Inc.

For specific information
Please call: (904) 278-5454
Fax: (904) 278-4366
Email: laddiebooksem@alltel.net
Toll Free 1-800-925-5454
Ask for Laddie Dwyer

Or Write:
The Rick Marino Fan Club
P.O. Box 16661
Jacksonville, Florida 32245-6661

UH, THANKYA, THANKYA VERY MUCH.

Photo Credits

Patty Carroll
Pages 3, 4, 17, 22, 23, 28. 29, 32, 33, 36, 43, 48, 51, 57, 58, 60, 65, 70, 71, 75, 77, 80, 106, 81, 101, 106, 111, 114, 115 & cover.

Travis Downs, It's All Good Photography
Pages 14, 16, 19, 20, 34, 37, 54, 55, 72, 86, & 88.

Shooting Star International Photo Agency, Hollywood, CA
Pages 5, 7, 8, 9, 12, 15, 27, 41, & 42.

All other images supplied by Rick Marino.

Acknowledgments

First of all, I would like to thank all of the folks I've had the privilege to perform for and, of course, I have to thank Elvis Presley, who made it all possible! He was truly one of a kind, the best of the best, trail-blazing, high-flying, and—without exception—the brightest of all superstars. "SHAZAM!!!"

My thanks to "THE BOYS"—Joe Rogers (my Chief of Security), Joe Coleman, Craig Craft, Brad Everly, Donny Ware, Tim Durdin, Todd Durdin, Barry Durdin, Wayne Pearson, Stuart Gregorey, Buddy Horne, John Stebbins, Bruce Fortenberry, Robert Fernandez, Jim "Mr." Wells, Ed "The Limoman" Liccardi, Butch & Don "Mr. Extraordinaire" Caudle, Dwight "The Genius" Braddy, Jeff & Gene Callahan, Danny & Johnny Spurgeon, Herb Blanton, Eddie Barfield, Jim Shortes, T.W. Gibbons, Johnny Rocks, Steve Hoye, Eric Olson, Doug Hodge, John Hamel, Dick McCarthy, Sal Zebouni, Steve Bridges, Doug McGinnis, Richard Yeomans, Victor Jones, Richard Smith, Jerry Ledbetter, Bo Knows Art, Shaun "Sherrill" Neilsen, and Mayor John Delaney.

My fan club—Shearlyn & Ginnie, Barbara & Jackie, Dottie & Judy, Marie & Phyliss, and all my fan club members, I sincerely thank you for all your years of support! Also, thanks to Lucy & Ann and the Elvis Always fan club.

My band—Lonnie Portwood, Mike Hammontree, Rick Fryfield, Tom Newton, Wayne Vige, Terry Jones, Danny Powell, Don Burris, Suzanne Stewart, Debbie Bailey Rider, Kelly Sisson, Larry Nader, Larry Cohen, Bob Sanders, Alan Wooldridge, and Jim Brown on sound.

Special thanks to the Van Dells—Stacy Todd, Doug Manley, Steve Ricks, and the rest of The Guys, including Merle & Ruth Dixon, John & Barb McKimm, Mary & Joe Quinn, and the Bellegambas – David, De De, Sue, Jeff, Tootsie, and Babe!

A very special thanks to Brother Dave Roberts, with whom I did my first performance as "The King," to Tom Carlile & The Craftsmen—

Don, Jerry, Terry, and Ray, who let me hang out with them and learn what it was all about. And, most of all, to my dad, Tony Marino, who has been an inspiration to me as I grew up watching him perform.

Thanks also to the Sparkmans—Gary & Vi, Judy, Brian, Linda, Sharon, and Shirley; the Browns—Herb, Rusty, Donna, Jane, and Lynn; the Moris—Wayne, Reiko, and Jimmy; the Kites—Judy, Margie, Patty, Roy, and the rest; Don & Dottie Curtis; Ron & Sandra Wahl; Gary & Connie Elliott; Leroy & Earline Kennon; Mike Falabella; Marti & Shelby McGinnis; the Hodges—Linda, Esther, Benjamin, Susan, Sharon, Charlie, & Joyce; Roger & Gail Olsen; John & Jerry Green; Gary Mayo & Sherry Spencer; My Pals in Masontown, PA.; Steve Bennett & The Boys at Big Chief; Dr. Woflson; Dr. C. Paul Wilcox & Staff; Dr. Silva & Romeu; Barbara & Earl Hoffay; Estus Charlie Joiner; Mark & Jackie Rowland Chambers; Gary Carnes; Ken White; Wendy Worth; Lisa & Linda Thornhill; Geneva Kovar; and Brenda & Mr. Barfield.

Thanks to people I have worked with: photographers John Church III, Ramon Hernandez, Roy Stoudemire, Patty Carroll, Travis Downs, Neal C. Lauron, Kent Barker, Stan Barone, Craig Larimer, Jon Peters, and Tom Spitz; hairstylists Vivian, Steve, Carlos, Tony, and Latifa; on the radio, Rob Robertson, Larry Browdy, and Al Albert (who did my first radio interview); from the press, Ann Hyman, Dan McDonald, Toni Trotti, Rick Grant, and Will at *The First Coast Entertainer*; agents Laddie Dwyer of A Unique Entertainment, Randy Scott, John Jelinick, Limeliters, and Mr. K.T. Chung; Wonda Vige (scarves); Will Reeb (costumes); Gary & Theresa Williams of Hanover Brass; Bill & Fran of Champion Printing; David at Xerographics; Mayor's Ed Austin & Jake Godbold; J. Erik Hart and The Florida Theatre; Eddie & Ruth Waller of Permaseal; Mike & Nancy Rowe; Jim Hannaford; Joe Carter of Graceland Records; Jim Rainey ("Whoa Jim!"); Shirley Schwebs of E.P. Continentals; Ron & Sandy Bessette; William "Bill" Henderson; David Winkler; Andrew Bergman; Nicolas Cage; Ruby Manis; Dean Martin; T.G. Shepperd and the guys; William White & the folks at TBS; D.J. Fontana & Karen; Los Super Ratones—Mario, Fernando, Oscar, & Joe; Tony Grova; Dr. Nasar-Polk Salad Sayegh; Teddy Washington; Henry "Tux" Vaught; Diamond Dallas Page; Darwin Lamb of E.I.F., Alison Herschberg and Travis Downs. Thank you.

And thanks to my family, Tony & Alice Marino; Larry & Jackie Clark; Betty Marino; Hazel, Pete, Patty, & Ginny Lubits; Rodney & Jennifer; the Diamonds—Rick, Stevie, Sherry, Jimmy, Aunt Lorraine, and Uncle Jim; the Martins—Ed, Aunt Mary, Judy, & family; Uncle Spike & Aunt Rose; the Mirabellas (especially Josephine); my sister Jody and her husband Mike; my nephew, Christopher Joseph Rubeis; my niece, Amy; my nephew, Bradley; and Faye Everly.